Category Killers

Category Killers

*The Retail Revolution
and Its Impact on
Consumer Culture*

Robert Spector

HARVARD BUSINESS SCHOOL PRESS
BOSTON, MASSACHUSETTS

Library of Congress Cataloging-in-Publication Data
Spector, Robert, 1947-
  Category killers : the retail revolution and its impact on consumer
culture / Robert Spector.
      p. cm.
  Includes bibliographical references.
  ISBN 1-57851-960-8
1. Shopping centers. 2. Retail trade. I. Title.
  HF5430.S67 2005
  658.8'7—dc22
                            2004012224

For Fae, a category of one.

Contents

Acknowledgments

First and foremost, I want to thank Jacqueline Murphy, editor extraordinaire, who first approached me about this idea. Jacque was my guide, taskmaster, and cheerleader; without her, this book would not have been possible nor as good.

A tip of the hat to Astrid Sandoval, editorial coordinator, who was always there in a pinch; and to Monica Jainschigg for her professional and insightful copyediting.

I gained tremendous insight from a wide variety of retail and development experts, most notably Robert DiNicola, retired chairman of Zale Corporation; Joseph H. Ellis of Goldman Sachs, Inc.; and Kemper Freeman, owner of the grand Bellevue Square shopping mall and a past chairman and current trustee of the International Council of Shopping Centers.

Elizabeth Wales, who has been my literary agent for fifteen years, has always been steadfast and perceptive—the perfect person to have in one's corner.

My daughter, Fae, makes me laugh and keeps me on my toes—often at the same time.

And my wife, Marybeth, somehow always gets me through the writing of a book—and this project was no exception. Thanks, dear. Let's do it again sometime.

Robert Spector
Seattle, Washington

Introduction

Look at all . . . this . . . stuff.

Outside the Home Depot store, a green and fuschia sea of little boxes of geraniums, impatiens, and pansies are surrounded by garden tools—manure forks, grass edgers, cultivators, and thatching rakes. A large sign proclaims free instructions on deck installations, with the choice of ten different styles and shapes. Inside the store, shoppers are surrounded by massive floor-to-ceiling shelves crammed with windows, hammers, drills, table saws—the list is virtually endless. Amid the buzzing of power saws, the beep-beep-beep of forklifts, and the jingle-jangle of nails, nuts, and bolts, there is a swarm of do-it-yourselfers of all shapes, sizes, ethnicities, desires, and aptitudes gathering their tools and materials like an army of insects constructing a shelter. Unlike the insects, if these workers have a question, they can get the answer from a man or woman clad in a bright orange apron.

Meanwhile, down the road at Toys "R" Us, a four-year-old Korean-American girl squeezes her mother's hand, as she edges closer to a box holding a Bratz Girl doll. With her index finger, she lightly touches the clear plastic that separates her from the doll. A few aisles down, an eight-year-old cranes his neck to gaze up at three levels of bicycles from Huffy, Mongoose, and Schwinn dangling from metal display beams. In another part of the store, a ten-year-old boy is begging his father for a Home

Depot Tool Box and Twelve-Piece Tool Set. We know where he will one day be spending his Saturday afternoons.

And so it goes: dozens of wide-screen flat-panel plasma television sets at Circuit City; rows of printers, copiers, and fax machines at OfficeMax; a parade of puppy food and toys at PETsMART; hundreds of thousands of books at Barnes & Noble. Today's shoppers are—depending on your point of view—either blessed or cursed by an overabundance—a surfeit, an engorgement, a glut—of stuff, amassed under one roof, in a retail concept that has had a profound impact on the consumer culture: category killers. Over the past two decades, category killers have dramatically altered our buying experience, becoming the most disruptive concept in retailing—and in everything that retailing touches.

Also known as "big-box" stores because of their mammoth footprint—twenty thousand square feet to more than one hundred thousand square feet—these retailers specialize in a distinct classification of merchandise such as toys, office supplies, home improvement—while offering everyday low prices and wide and deep inventories. They earned the sobriquet "category killer" because their goal is to dominate the category and kill the competition—whether it be mom-and-pop stores, smaller regional chains, or general merchandise stores that cannot compete on price and/or selection.

Category killers and Wal-Mart (more about this giant later) have helped expand and upscale the "mass market" by aggressively driving down the prices of goods and services, and making affordable what were once upscale products such as laptop computers, big-screen TVs, or designer apparel. Today, virtually every one of us—regardless of income—is part of the ever-expanding mass market, where the differences among stores—Dollar Stores to Kmart to Macy's—are measured in slight gradations. A discount store like Target, which employs its own in-house designers, has made even fashion merchandise just another affordable commodity. (Wal-Mart is now trying to do the same.) Consequently, loyalty to a particular store has become a casualty of our changing consumer culture. At one time, shoppers used to identify with a store, just as they identified with the make of the car they drove. Today, many of us simply want more and better goods, and we will shop the retailer that provides those goods at a price that we consider "affordable."

As they fight to insure their own survival in a world of retail Darwinism, category killers have gone through their own evolution.

In the beginning, because they required literally acres of parking, pioneer category killers such as Toys "R" Us and Home Depot located in undeveloped or underdeveloped areas with plenty of open space. For many years, the interiors of these stores were devoid of inviting design and amenities; they were no-frills zones in cookie-cutter, single-floor buildings. In exchange for Spartan surroundings, these retailers offered low prices and convenience for busy time-starved shoppers. The strategy was simple: Pile it high and sell it cheap.

But in recent years, spurred by competition both within and without the category, the best category killers have become more consumer-centric, adjusting their look and feel to better serve and sell to the customer. Even the most bare-bones big-box store has had to upgrade signage, product presentation, and even (gasp!) customer service. Most have added related product lines, such as Home Depot's move into the home-appliance business.

PETsMART, which was founded for the purpose of selling food and other pet-related products, has evolved, in the company's view, into a tool to assist owners in providing total lifetime care for their pets. Key to this strategy has been rethinking and redesigning the physical store itself. Originally, the company merchandised its goods in various sections such as food or hard goods. Today, PETsMART stores are built around pet categories (i.e., a cat section, a dog section, etc.) and feature a more open layout that is consumer-friendly and reflects how today's pet owner thinks, shops, and lives.

The nature of the specialization has changed, from products with similar characteristics of distribution or usage to products grouped around a lifestyle characteristic. For example, bookstores compete against Amazon.com and Wal-Mart by transforming themselves into browsing rooms and coffee shops with wireless Internet sites. They offer an experience that appeals to a highly mobile, higher-income consumer.

With several retailers competing in virtually every category, we will be limiting our discussion here to a few major ones in a select group of categories: toys, books, office supplies, home improvement, consumer electronics, and pets. In each category, there are only two or three players of any significance. Each of them has been influenced by the man who gave the world the category killer: Charles Lazarus of Toys "R" Us.

Also included is one non-big-box retailer: Starbucks Coffee, which created its category and has redefined the world's notion of java. Instead of building one big store in a neighborhood, Starbucks bunches several stores within close proximity of each other, whether across the street, down the block, around the corner—all over town. Unlike the other category killers that drive down the prices of the product in its category, Starbucks has raised the price, single-handedly creating a mass market for gourmet coffee that never before existed. Starbucks has taken an "affordable luxury" and made it available for everyone from students to truck drivers to CEOs. Regardless of income level, at Starbucks we all drink from the same metaphorical cup.

Although the focus of this book is on specialized retailers, a discussion of the transformation of consumer culture would be incomplete without considering the impact of Wal-Mart Stores, Inc., the giant general merchandise discounter (and its rival Target), and Costco, the member warehouse chain (and its antagonist Wal-Mart's Sam's Club). They take huge bites out of category killers—Wal-Mart sells more toys than Toys "R" Us; Costco moves more books—particularly deeply discounted bestsellers—than Barnes & Noble. As the biggest corporation in the world, with $256.3 billion in sales in 2003 (close to 2.5 percent of America's gross national product), Wal-Mart has an impact—either directly or indirectly—on virtually every other type of retail and retail-vendor business on the planet.

THIS BOOK IS DIVIDED into three parts. Part One includes an explanation of category killers and where they fit in the evolution of modern retailing. Chapter 1 is a description of what big-box retail looks like on the ground, specifically in an area south of Seattle that has become home for virtually every existing category killer. What was once verdant land is now covered with black top and bricks and mortar. How and why did that transformation take place? And how is the metamorphosis of this area a reflection what is happening in other parts of the country? Chapter 2 looks at the rise of discounting in the United States, which set the stage for Charles Lazarus and Toys "R" Us. Chapter 3 investigates retailers who took a page out of the Lazarus playbook and expanded the category-killer concept to office supplies, pet products, home improvements, and other product classifications.

Part Two explains how and why these retailers have come to dominate their categories. In this section, we will investigate the gestalt of category killers and their impact on the cultural landscape of Main Street America (as well as Canada, South America, Europe, and Asia). We will look at their effect on small specialty stores, mom-and-pop stores, regional chains, small-town downtowns, department stores, discount stores, supermarkets, and traditional shopping centers. These days, category killers are often grouped together in malls dubbed "power centers," which draw customers from miles away and, in the process, alter our traditional concept of "neighborhood." We used to walk around our neighborhood; now we drive to it.

Expansion—both domestically and abroad—is the economic imperative of every one of the category killers; if they do not grow, they die. In the search for growth, we will see how retail sales taxes generated by category killers and big-box general merchandise stores influence the land-use decisions of local governments, be they in Cypress, California, or New York City. By luring a Wal-Mart, Home Depot, or Costco to produce sales taxes, local governments can often avoid having to raise property taxes and other levies on existing residents and businesses. In Lancaster, California, for example, sales taxes from the local Costco store contributes more than half a million dollars every year to the city's $33 million budget, providing enough money to pay for all the city's recreation programs, or the net cost of the performing arts center, or all discretionary law enforcement operations, such as stings.

Part Three covers category killers' need to expand their reach to urban, suburban, and rural areas, and the challenges they face in maintaining their competitive edge, both in their ability to grow and in their dexterity in fending off challengers. We will also see that their aggressive expansion strategies have led to the inevitable backlash, as many local governments, under pressure from local and national anti-sprawl activists, land-use experts, and competing independent retailers, take a closer look at the toll of these stores on land-use legislation, farmland, taxation, migration patterns, traffic patterns, infrastructure, wages, and jobs—the ones they add and the ones they take away (by eliminating other retailers). Independent shopkeepers have been fighting back by forming grass-roots opposition groups.

This opposition is not surprising. There has always been hostility to disruptive retail concepts. Over the past 150 years, at one time or another, there has been vigorous resistance to department stores, mail-order catalogs, shopping malls, discounters, and chain stores of any kind. Because each of those retailing ideas subverted the then–business as usual, opponents felt those disruptive retailers had to be contravened by whatever means necessary: lawsuits, state and federal legislation, or pressure on vendors not to sell to whatever new interloper came along. The latest "villain" is the category killer.

ON A PERSONAL NOTE, I have been involved in retail since I was a small child. My father owned and operated a butcher shop in a small outdoor farmers market in Perth Amboy, New Jersey. My mother, sisters, uncle, and cousins all worked there at one time or another. I remember as a young boy going with my parents to the A&P supermarket, which was a couple of blocks away from the farmers market. While my mother shopped the aisles, my dad would station himself at the meat case, checking out A&P's prices on flank steak, pork chops, and the like. At the time, I didn't fully appreciate all the implications, but A&P had my dad's little business in its crosshairs. He was able to survive because he offered his customers good products at a competitive price—plus a lot of personalized customer service.

And yet, these giant retailers wouldn't be successful unless they satisfied certain consumer needs, whether for ten different kinds of printer-fax-scanner-copiers at Staples, or a cotton/nylon "comfort harness" (available in small, medium and large) for your pet ferret at PETsMART.

My first job out of college in 1969, was writing newspaper advertising copy for the Bamberger's department store chain, the New Jersey division of Macy's. Bamberger's flagship store on Market Street in Newark, was a classic, venerable big-city department store, eight floors chock full of suits, dresses, mattresses, couches, lamps, stereos, books, toys, candy. Although I didn't particularly like my job, I always experienced a special feeling walking into the store before opening hours, taking the escalator (never the elevator) up to the advertising department offices on the eighth floor, and being surrounded by all this stuff. Perhaps I was influenced by a movie I loved as a kid, called *One Touch of Venus*. In this adaptation of a Broadway musical written by S. J. Perelman, Kurt Weill, and Ogden Nash, a shy department-store window-trimmer kisses a statue of Venus, which brings her to life. As the window-trimmer and Venus (Ava Gardner) hide in the department store after closing, we see how everything one might ever need in life is right there in that store.

If *One Touch of Venus* were remade today, it wouldn't even be set in a department store, but rather in a Wal-Mart (today's version of the department store); this is what happens in the film *One From The Heart*, in which the pregnant heroine, abandoned by her boyfriend, sets up house in a Wal-Mart (which has everything she needs: food, diapers, toys, etc.) before being discovered, and then celebrated in the media. Wal-Mart is more of a cultural icon today than any department store will ever be again.

A constant theme of this book is that retail and consumer culture are always evolving. Retailing in a free market is always fluid. Concepts, locations, population migrations, tastes, brands, pricing, and executive leadership are forever in motion. Formats borrow from other formats; category killers branch out to carry other categories. Today, more than ever before, if a retailer is slow, it will be devoured by the swift; if it is ineffective, it will be outmaneuvered by the efficient. That's what makes retailing exhilarating and terrifying. There's no level ground in retail; it's either up or down. It's a business in which you get a new report card every day. In retail, as they tell you in the fine print of a mutual fund prospectus, past performance is no guarantee of future success.

In the meantime, let's go shopping.

PART I

The Colossal Competitors

1

From Cow Pastures to Category Killers

There is nothing wrong with change,
if it is in the right direction.

—Winston Churchill

THE JET-BLACK PAVEMENT of Southcenter Parkway slices a path through an expanse of commercial sprawl ten miles south of downtown Seattle, Washington. On one side of this land is the convergence of two major highways—Interstate 5 and Interstate 405; and on the other side is the bustling, upscale Southcenter Mall, where the Nordstrom, J.C. Penney, and Bon-Macy's department stores anchor the 1.3-million-square-foot shopping center, which was built in 1968 by the real-estate arm of Allied Stores, then one of the most powerful forces in department stores and shopping centers.

Just to the north of Southcenter Mall are Toys "R" Us, Target, and the Bon-Macy's clearance store. Adjacent to that group of stores is the 450,000-square-foot Parkway Supercenter. Parkway is a "power center" of category killers and specialty stores, which are grouped together and share a common parking lot: Best Buy electronics, Babies "R" Us, CompUSA, Gart Sports, Pier 1 Imports, Party City, Old Navy, Hallmark Cards, Bath & Body Works, Cost Plus Imports, Marshall's, Ross, David's Bridal, and Starbucks. The Supercenter also features a twelve-screen multiplex movie theater and a half-dozen chain restaurants, including Applebee's, Red Robin, Outback Steakhouse, and Sizzler. Across the street from Parkway Supercenter are Borders Books & Music, Office Max, PETs-MART, Linens 'n Things, and Jo-Ann, Etc. (fabrics, crafts, and decorating and sewing products). Less than a mile to the west of Southcenter Mall are Barnes & Noble, Circuit City, Home Depot, Lowe's Home Improvement Warehouse, The Good Guys, Office Depot, and Bed Bath & Beyond. This entire area is also sprinkled with furniture stores such as Ethan Allen, Thomasville, Bassett, and The Bon Furniture Gallery.

This is a cars-only zone. Anyone seen actually walking along busy, four-lane Southcenter Parkway is either delirious or has run out of gas.

All of these stores are located in the 8.3-square-mile city of Tukwila, population 17,000. This area, which has little nearby residential space, and relatively little office space, is typical of the hegemony of retail that is being played out all over the United States as well as in many parts of the world. Its development is a case study in how big retail has become a driving force in land use, municipal tax bases, and the evolution of the concept of neighborhood.

Hazelnuts to Home Depot

The land that would ultimately become a huge commercial hub was "settled" in the mid-nineteenth century when the first non–Native Americans arrived in the region, which was then dominated by the Duwamish tribe. The terrain is criss-crossed by several rivers, and the valleys that surround them. The White River and the Green River rushed out of the Cascade Mountains to the east, meeting in the southeast in an area known as Auburn (now the home of a Super Mall). The Green River met the Black River, an outflow from Lake Washington, near what is today the city of Tukwila (whose name in local Native American dialect means "land where the hazelnuts grow"). Those two rivers formed the Duwamish River, which flows north toward Seattle into Elliott Bay. Native Americans made their homes along the Duwamish and Black Rivers, where they resided in cedar longhouses nestled in verdant groves of hazelnut trees. The Duwamish were the first "retailers" in the area. As hunters, fishers, and farmers, they operated up and down the river, trading their goods with neighboring tribes.

By the 1860s, non–Native Americans were hauling coal, produce, and livestock on seventy-foot flat-bottomed riverboats along the rivers from Seattle to Auburn and back. Back then, Seattle, which today is a fifteen-minute drive away, was a two-day journey by boat.

By the beginning of the twentieth century, the lush green fields of the river valleys accommodated large herds of dairy cattle for a burgeoning milk-production industry. Although the initial wave of newcomers comprised primarily emigrants from Europe, the 1900 census included thirteen Japanese families, who accounted for 118 people living in the White River Valley. Those pioneering Japanese workers cleared land and harvested crops for the European-American farmers, who paid them about a dollar a day for a ten-hour workday. A few Japanese workers began farming on their own, raising potatoes, strawberries, cabbage, bunch carrots, hothouse rhubarb, raspberries, and blackberries.

When the price of milk declined after World War I, many Japanese dairy farmers switched to raising vegetables and berries, which they sold out of the back of their trucks every Saturday at places like the Pike Place Market in Seattle, and supplied to other regional food outlets.

In 1907, the U.S. government began to limit the number of Japanese permitted to settle in this country. Sixteen years later, the Anti-Alien Land Law barred immigrants from owning land. Although ineligible for U.S. citizenship, those families that had a child born in America were allowed to own the land by putting the deed in the name of their *nisei* (American-born) child. By 1930, some two hundred Japanese families were farming in the White River valley to the south of the Duwamish. In 1942, after the attack on Pearl Harbor, citizens of Japanese descent in the White River Valley were removed from their land and taken to the War Relocation Camp at Tule Lake, California. At the conclusion of the war, most of them lost their farms and personal belongings; only about thirty Japanese-American families returned to the valley area to resume farming.

The next dominant Asian immigrant group was Filipinos, who arrived after the war to farm the southern part of the valley. They were primarily "truck gardeners" who sold their fresh produce and vegetables at Seattle-area markets and/or roadside stands.

The combination of the valley's abundance of rivers and the region's characteristic rainfall meant that virtually every year the rivers flooded the valley farmland and the small towns that had been sprouting up along the rivers since the early 1900s. To regulate the river waters and hold back the flood waters, in 1963 the Army Corps of Engineers built the Howard A. Hanson Dam in the Eagle Gorge of the upper Green River. This engineering feat created a productive habitat for fish, particularly Chinook salmon. With floods no longer a factor, farming prospered.

But then the law of unintended consequences took over. As the population of the region grew, businesses began looking for less expensive land outside the city of Seattle. Lo and behold, here was the Green Valley and its miles of flat, treeless, open—and now floodless—acreage, which provided easy access to the tracks of the Northern Pacific Railway (now owned by Burlington Northern) and the Chicago, Milwaukee and St. Paul (now part of the Union Pacific Railroad). Freight trains passed through the little hamlet of Kent on their way north to Seattle or south to Tacoma.

Ample acreage that was easily accessible by rail, truck, or automobile was attractive. Farm families, faced with rising land prices and skyrocketing property taxes, began selling off their acreage to developers; so did corporate landowners, including the railroads. Soon, where crops once flourished, there grew a great network of warehouses and distribution centers. In 1965, the Boeing Aerospace Company located the first of several major facilities in the area. Many electronics and technology firms followed suit.

At the same time, in the early 1960s, the region added Interstate 5, which stretched from the Canadian border to the Mexican border. By the end of the decade, it was crossed by Interstate 405, creating a convergence of the region's primary freeways. This was where the Southcenter shopping center was built by Allied Stores Corporation, the successor to Hahn Department Stores, Inc., which owned Jordan Marsh, Maas Brothers, Stern's, and The Bon Marché.

Allied and other developers of regional malls were greatly aided by the federal government's construction of the interstate highway system in the 1950s. Officially called the Dwight D. Eisenhower System of Interstate and Defense Highways (Eisenhower was president at the time), the system was intended to make it easier and more efficient for manufacturers to distribute their products throughout the country.

Because this time period coincided with the tensions of the Cold War being fought between the United States and the Soviet Union, supporters claimed that the superhighway system was warranted because it would be essential for the rapid and orderly transportation of military equipment and personnel. The 42,793 miles of road did more than that—they accelerated the suburbanization of America. As R. Dean Wolfe of the May Department Stores Company, stated in the book *America's Marketplace*, "When Eisenhower put the highway in place, he didn't realize he was destroying downtown."[1]

A Different Kind of Crop

Today, in the area around Southcenter, black soil has been replaced by blacktop, and much of what grows in the valley is retailers. There are now some four million square feet of retail space in the Southcenter area, supporting the people who work in the neighboring eighty million square feet of office and industrial space, the guests staying in dozens of hotels, and the 247,000 inhabitants (with an average annual income of more than $70,000) within a five-mile radius. The retail at Southcenter actually draws customers from as far as twenty miles away. With the restaurants and movie theaters, the Parkway Supercenter attracts nightlife, which enables the stores to extend their hours. Welcome to the new neighborhood.

And why not? Retail space commands triple the value of the light industrial space that once dominated the Valley after farming was phased out. This change in direction has been a boon to the municipalities in which most of this retail is located—the towns of Renton (which boasts IKEA, Wal-Mart, and Fry's Electronics) and Tukwila, which changed their zoning laws to encourage the building of more stores and to harvest a bumper crop of retail sales taxes.

Emblematic of the changes in the area is the eight-acre plot of land directly across from Parkway Supercenter. Back in 1978, The Boeing Company built a nine-story office building on the property to house one of its divisions. In the early 1990s, when it was going through one of its cyclical downsizings, the aerospace giant sold the property to Michael Sandorffy, a Seattle developer, for $20 million. The office market in general in this, the southern end of Seattle, had dried up, and this particular building turned out to be a white elephant with outdated mechanical systems and oversized floors. Unable to rent out the building, Sandorffy razed it and replaced it with Parkplace Center, a 160,000-square-foot shopping center of category killers, including Borders Books & Music, Office Max, and The Sports Authority—the ideal complement to the Parkway Supercenter.

Today, with retail space so valuable, light industry (such as warehouses and distribution centers) is moving farther and farther south to previously undeveloped or underdeveloped rural areas of the state, which eliminated its internal distribution tax to attract investment from out-of-state retail chains. In rural Lacey, Home Depot is building a 750,000-square-foot warehouse on forty-four acres; and Target Corporation is constructing a 1.5-million-square-foot distribution center on 122 acres. The two projects represent nine hundred jobs in areas that desperately need them. Although, thanks to a farmland preservation act, some farming does remain in the various river valleys south of Seattle, eventually new homes will be built, the population will grow, and those once sparsely populated areas will be big enough to attract their own shopping malls and/or power centers. And so it goes.

What has happened—and will continue to happen—in this area south of Seattle is being repeated in virtually every corner of the United States and in burgeoning retail markets in Mexico, Canada, South America, and Asia.

How did this happen? How did big-box category killers come to dominate the landscape and forever alter the way we shop?

2

Charles Lazarus
and the Birth of the
Category Killer

In business, the competition will bite you
if you keep running; if you stand still,
they will swallow you.

**— William Knudsen, Jr., Chairman,
Ford Motor Company**

FOR MOST of the first two decades of the twentieth century, department stores put very little emphasis on selling toys. The youth culture that would come to full bloom in the 1950s was a few decades away. Still, there were a handful of canny retailers who saw that the children's business was going to be a developing market. Those retailers were supported by experts in child behavior, who proclaimed that children needed activities and products to keep them amused and occupied, particularly when they were out of school on summer vacation. Of course, children have always had special needs, but they used to rely on themselves or their parents to create their diversions. By the mid-1920s the United

States had become the world's leading manufacturer of toys and playthings for the backyard, the beach, and the campground—for the "little private room, which every child desperately needs to fulfill his or her individuality," according to a December 1928 issue of *Toy World* magazine. "Play is the child's business; toys the material with which he works."[1]

In 1928, the brothers Jesse and Percy Straus, who co-owned Macy's—"The World's Largest Store"—on 34th Street and Broadway in New York City, jumped on the new toy craze and arranged a major "exposition" of thousands of playthings, at which energetic demonstrators showed how the toys worked. (Seventy-five years later, and ten blocks farther up Broadway, Toys "R" Us did the same thing, with a four-level, 110,000-square foot store at Times Square.) To underscore the educational reasons for buying these items, the Strauses hired eminent child behaviorists who expounded on why children should have toys—specifically the toys sold at Macy's. To further stimulate the toy market, Macy's became the multimedia Walt Disney Company of its day—the retailer published kids' magazines and produced and sponsored kids' radio shows, which were always pushing secret decoder rings and other such delights. Most important, Macy's installed what is considered the first year-round toy area in a department store, in which in-store toy shows and demonstrations were staged. Other retailers around the country followed suit, devoting considerable time, effort, and space to amuse little Dick and Jane, and to stimulate their parents to buy them *that* toy.

From then on, department stores, led by Sears, Roebuck and Co., dominated the toy category—particularly around holiday time, when they generated most of their sales. Macy's, which would eventually house the single largest toy department in the country, unofficially introduced the holiday season with its Thanksgiving Day parade, which was highlighted by the season's first sighting of Santa Claus. (This was in the days before advertisers began hawking their Christmas wares in mid-October.) The film *Miracle on 34th Street*, which was set in a fictionalized version of Macy's, became a cinema classic. The Montgomery Ward chain contributed to American popular culture the character of Rudolph the Red-Nosed Reindeer, the creation of an anonymous writer in Ward's advertising department for use in a 1939 Christmas give-away program. (Having once toiled in the advertising department of a department store, where I wrote newspaper advertisements for Christmas toys, I salute that unacknowledged copywriter.)

At holiday time, department stores across the nation pulled out all the stops when it came to displaying and romanticizing their toy selection. In Seattle, for example, Frederick & Nelson was *the* place to have your picture taken sitting on Santa Claus's lap and to view remarkable window displays. In 1952, director of design Joe Sjursen hired a retired Navy engineer to teach him a new technology—perfected by the Navy—to power electrical devices with body heat. Sjursen used the system to propel an electric toy train that was part of an elaborate Christmas display in the store's most prominent window. When a window shopper on the street pressed her hand to a spot marked on the window, the warmth of the hand activated a transformer that started the trains into gear—and stopped them when the hand was removed. Sjursen's device, which became a Frederick & Nelson Christmas tradition, was typical of the kind of creativity that department stores were once noted for, in the merchandising and selling categories that they once dominated.[2]

Everything in the toy business changed with the arrival of Charles Lazarus. He revolutionized the way that toys were popularly sold and started a movement that led to the dismantling, piece by piece, of the categories that once made a department store a *department* store.

Lazarus was born in 1923, in the back room of his father's bicycle shop in Washington, D.C. The senior Lazarus's business consisted primarily of buying broken bicycles, rebuilding them, and then selling them. "I always wondered why we didn't sell new bicycles," he told *Atlantic Monthly*. "My father said it was because the big chain stores could sell them so much cheaper than we could."[3]

That fact of retail life made a lasting impression on Lazarus. Upon returning from service in World War II, where he had served as a cryptographer, Lazarus, then twenty-five years old, felt he was too old to start college, but old enough to start a business. Investing $5,000 of his own money, he took over his father's shop, liquidated the bicycles, and replaced them with baby furniture. The idea was to tap into the so-called baby boom by catering to his fellow veterans, who were returning home from the war to start families.

It was a good business but, after running the shop for a few years, Lazarus realized that there were limitations: Baby furniture doesn't wear out. What kind of children's product *does* wear out (or is discarded because of boredom)? *Toys.* After a sufficient number of customers came into the store asking for toys, Lazarus decided to get into that business. He renamed his new store the Children's Supermart (the r's in the logo were reversed to grab attention), which was built around big selection and good value. Lazarus's idea was to offer brand-name toys at below list price. At the time, U.S. consumers were coping with steadily rising prices, thanks to a run-up in inflation in the aftermath of the war. Canny merchants knew there was money to be made selling products below list prices and operating on low margins—discounting.

To place into context what Toys "R" Us accomplished, here is a look at the evolution of discount.

The War Against Discounting

"One of the accepted axioms of selling is that when demand is created for a type of marketing institution, one will arise to satisfy that demand. The discount store was just such a response," observed Penrose Scull in *From Peddlers to Merchant Princes: A History of Selling in America.*[4]

Discounting, which had been around in some form since the 1930s, had some very powerful opponents, comprising a fascinating combination of strange bedfellows. First of all, in order to understand the hostility to discounting, we must examine the opposition to big chain stores. There was strong, vocal sentiment in many parts of the country against these giant retailers, which were criticized for using their purchasing clout to destroy small, independent retailers that could not wrangle the same kinds of deals, discounts, and terms from manufacturers. In the 1920s, the anti-chain forces included nearly three hundred local or national organizations, which boasted more than eight million members, or almost 7 percent of the current population of the United States. Some populist politicians based their reelection campaigns on their antipathy to chains. Governor Huey P. Long, the notorious "Kingfish" of Louisiana, declared that he would rather his state be occupied by thieves and gangsters than operators of chain stores.

A typical example of this sentiment is found in the following excerpt from a 1922 book, *Meeting Chain Store Competition*:

> *Every retailer who has to meet chain store competition thinks he needs no one to tell him what a chain store is. To him it is a cut-rate competitor managed from the outside by a soul-less corporation. What the principles behind it may be he neither knows nor cares. He is confronted with conditions, not theories, with the necessity for keeping trade which shows a persistent tendency to drift over to the chain store which shouts loudly and continually for business with colored window banners and multitudinous price cards.*[5]

The only thing missing from that message is *The Music Man*'s Professor Harold Hill alerting the townsfolk of "trouble right here in River City."

Throughout the 1930s, individual states enacted special taxes targeted at the big chain stores, which accounted for more than 60 percent of the more than four thousand department stores in the country. The remaining 40 percent were still local and independent. On the federal level, in response to the Great Depression, the U.S. Congress tried to control the economy with the creation of the National Recovery Administration (NRA), which sought to establish sets of rules for every aspect of American commerce, including working hours, wages, trade practices and, of course, prices. Although the Supreme Court would eventually declare the NRA unconstitutional, federal lawmakers were not done with meddling.

At the forefront of the fight was Representative Wright Patman, a New Deal Democrat and economic populist from Texarkana, Texas. Working with Senator Joseph Taylor Robinson, a Democrat from Arkansas, Patman helped pass the 1936 Robinson-Patman Act; this supplemented the Clayton Antitrust Act of 1914, which was itself an amendment to the Sherman Antitrust Act of 1890. Congressman Henry De Lamar Clayton's 1914 bill sought to eliminate so-called predatory price cutting by prohibiting chain stores from entering into exclusive sales contracts with manufacturers. Robinson-Patman, which was also known as the Anti-Chain Store Act, made it unlawful for any person or firm involved in interstate commerce to charge different consumers a different price for the same commodity when the effect would be "to substantially lessen competition" or to create a monopoly. (The legislation did not include apparel because that product category had too many variables—styles, degrees of quality, etc.—for anyone to be able to come up with a strict set of workable rules and discernible criteria.)

Although it was intended to protect independent retailers, Robinson-Patman also had the support of wholesalers. These middlemen in the commercial continuum considered Robinson-Patman a guarantee of job security because it prevented the powerful chains from purchasing goods directly from manufacturers for lower prices. But by fixing the wholesale prices for goods, the numerous federal and state so-called fair trade laws compelled retailers to charge fixed minimum prices that were set—and enforced—by the manufacturers of the product. The problem with that thinking was that the chains and the manufacturers could privately agree upon a price for an item, which still gave the chains an advantage over independents.

Wright Patman, who would eventually become the powerful chairman of the House Banking and Currency Committee, didn't want to merely retard the chains; he made it clear that he wanted to drive the large ones out of business. In 1938, he introduced legislation, nicknamed "the chain death sentence bill," that proposed a series of onerous taxes on chain stores. Under the Patman formula, the more stores it owned, the more the retailer would have had to pay in taxes.

Earl Sams, then the president of the J.C. Penney department store, spoke for his colleagues when he warned that the elimination of national chains would be a financial burden on the American family and would lead to the destruction of small towns. Offering the same argument that category killers submit today, Sams declared that, compared with independent stores, the chains paid more local taxes, better wages, and higher rents.[6] The chain-store industry fought back with political donations to Patman's opponents and waged public relations campaigns to sway a consuming public that didn't need much convincing; they *liked* shopping at chain stores. Patman's bill was killed in committee and never came to a vote on the floor. Eventually, the Supreme Court saw the folly in the fair trade laws. Beginning with a 1951 decision on minimum-price agreements, the court ruled that rather than promoting competition, price-fixing *stifled* competition and promoted a distribution monopoly.

Discounting Cashes In

Some canny independent retailers found ways to get into discounting.[7] One of the trailblazers was Eugene Ferkauf, whose father owned and operated a couple of luggage stores in midtown Manhattan in the 1930s and 1940s. Returning home after serving as a Signal Corps sergeant during World War II, Ferkauf was soon attracted to the nascent business of discount retailing. His inspiration was a fellow New Yorker named Charles Wolf, who had been running a wholesale luggage business in downtown Manhattan since the late 1940s. While selling his wares to his retail customers at the traditional markup, he also handed out his business card to select customers, who could visit his storage space and buy luggage pieces at a discounted price. Because he was not *strictly* a retailer, Wolf got around the Robinson-Patman Act.

In 1948, Ferkauf opened his first discount store on 46th Street near Fifth Avenue in Manhattan, which he named E.J. Korvette. (The name came from "E" for Eugene, "J" for friend Joe Zwillenberg; "Korvette" was a take on the Canadian WWII fighting ship, the *Corvette*.) The retail operation offered discounted appliances, televisions, razors, and other hard goods and was called a "membership store"—not open to the general public—and thus immune from Robinson-Patman. The store was on the second floor of the building, which gave it a low profile. But on the street, Ferkauf's employees distributed membership cards to passersby, who were eligible to buy items at discounts of up to 33 percent. By 1954, there were five Korvette's stores in Manhattan, and one in suburban Hempstead, New York.

Competing full-line retailers such as Gimbel's and Macy's called for strict enforcement of the fair trade laws. Like most established retailers, they looked on discounters such as Ferkauf with disdain, branding them "parasites" and "bootleggers" (and those were the nice names). They filed several dozen fair trade suits against Ferkauf, but most were dismissed. Ferkauf actually benefited from the suits, which were widely covered in the New York newspapers, thereby providing Korvette's, which did no advertising, with lots of free publicity. What New Yorker could resist buying goods at discount prices?

By this time, everybody in the New York metropolitan area knew about Korvette's. Sales mushroomed in the 1950s, rising from $55 million a year to $750 million a year over a ten-year period. At one point in the early 1960s, Korvette's was opening one huge new store every seven weeks, reaching a peak of forty-five stores in nine metropolitan areas. Ferkauf, whom the press dubbed "The Duke of Discounting," even made the cover of *Time*—to this day, a rarity for a retailer, unless your name is Jeff Bezos (amazon.com) or Meg Whitman (eBay). Korvette's later went through a series of management and ownership changes before being liquidated in 1980.

MARTIN CHASE was an unsung, but profoundly influential discounting pioneer who, in the early 1950s, was running a gift-ribbon manufacturing business in a small space in the old Ann & Hope weaving mill in Cumberland, Rhode Island. Faced with overwhelming competition from the 3M Company, which could produce gift ribbon more efficiently and cheaply than he ever could, Chase wisely explored other business opportunities. While he was looking, his father suggested he find a way to liquidate his existing inventory of ribbon. So, in 1953, Chase set up what was intended to be a temporary operation in a small space on the third floor of the Ann & Hope mill. The operation was completely self-service (a portent of Toys "R" Us); customers gathered up the goods, put them in bags, and paid on their way out. Amazed by the popularity of the concept and the fast turnover of goods, Chase and his son, Irwin, soon added housewares, greeting cards, and hosiery, and then opened up the business, which they called Ann & Hope, to the general public. They later moved their operation to a five-thousand-square-foot space in the basement, where they added health and beauty aids, domestics, bedding, and furniture, all sold at low prices.

Many retailers made pilgrimages to Cumberland, Rhode Island, to visit the Ann & Hope store and talk to the Chases to see if they could emulate the concept. One visitor was Harry Blair Cunningham, then vice president (and later president) of the SS Kresge five-and-ten-cent store chain. At the time, Kresge was suffering sluggish sales and sagging profits because most of its seven hundred stores were in downtown areas that were being abandoned by the middle class for the suburbs. The job of solving the problem was put in the hands of the fifty-year-old Cunningham, who had been working for Kresge since graduating college, starting out as a stock boy.

For two years, beginning in 1957, Cunningham traveled all over the country to study both the Kresge operation and its competition. By the time he became president in 1959, he had decided upon a new direction for Kresge: selling branded, nationally advertised merchandise at a discount.

Cunningham believed that Kresge could make the transition because it boasted several key advantages over established small regional chains: a strong organization, an army of experienced store managers, and a sophisticated real estate department that was adept at locating lower-cost freestanding sites away from high-rent shopping centers, which would keep down overhead expenses. The acceptance of Cunningham's recommendations by the Kresge board was proof that the man was a convincing salesman. Kresge's bold decision was then, and remains today, a rarity for a major national retailer—to completely redefine its business plan. The new discount stores were called "K-Mart" (the hyphen was later dropped).

Although it was a general merchandise retailer, Kmart helped create the template for category killers. Based on convenience, quality, and price, Kmart provided cost-conscious and time-conscious customers a one-stop shopping center where they could purchase brand-name general merchandise, primarily through self-service. Unlike department stores, Kmarts had only one set of entrance/exit doors and just a single, centralized check-out area located at the front. Low prices were achieved by quickly turning over inventory. Kmart stores were not part of malls, but rather placed on stand-alone sites with huge parking lots to serve car-dependent suburbanites. Kmart preferred the stand-alone sites because it was not interested in having any competitor stores close by. As Harry Cunningham said in 1970, "Our stores are miniature one-stop shopping centers. If our merchandise assortment is right, we are in a position to take care of the needs of the typical American family. So we don't need another group of stores beside us to dilute the traffic flow into our store."[8]

One could interpret Cunningham's remarks as either confident or arrogant, but those words foretell the kind of insular thinking that would eventually cause Kmart's downfall.

Sam Walton, the founder of Wal-Mart Stores, Inc., was probably the most noteworthy visitor to Ann & Hope. Irwin Chase recalled that his father told Walton, "if he had low enough overhead, he could sell very cheap."[9] (He sure got that one right!) At the time, Walton was operating fourteen franchise stores in the Ben Franklin retail chain, which he wanted to convert to discount operations. When he couldn't convince the corporate heads at Ben Franklin to make that move, Walton went off on his own, opening his first independent Wal-Mart Discount City in Rogers, Arkansas, in 1962—the same year that saw the debuts of Kmart, Target Stores, and Woolco (a division of F.W. Woolworth, the first successful five-and-ten-cent store).

The Heyday of Discounting

Discounting was built on a simple formula: Sell brand-name apparel, shoes, toys, electronics, records, etc., in a low-overhead

store—some as large as 110,000 square feet—that would enable the retailer to charge prices below those of department
and specialty stores. The times were ripe for discounting. In
the early and mid-1970s, the United States was hit hard by a
Middle East oil embargo, which added to already soaring
inflation and ended the nearly three decades of economic
boom times that began with the end of the World War II.
With department stores having to deal with skyrocketing
overhead expenses that could not always be offset by rising
prices, strapped consumers turned to discounters, with their
low prices, strong buying power, efficient technology (logis-
tic and information), and wide and deep inventories.

As American families migrated to the suburbs, discounters
followed them. Discounters took advantage of improved
highways and free parking to draw customers from within a
five-mile radius in urban areas and a twenty-five-mile radius
in rural areas. Soon, virtually every region of the country had
its own local discount operation: Spartan, Zayres, Mammoth
Mart, The Giant Store, Bradlees, Shopper's World, Two Guys,
W.T. Grant, and others. Neiman Marcus these stores were
not; their décor was cheap looking, with interior walls covered in paint colors usually not found in nature. But consumers didn't care; they were more than willing to exchange
ambience for cheap prices. In fact, if the store did not look
good, consumers felt more confident that they were getting a
better value. By this time, the American consumer had become accustomed to shopping in big spaces, thanks to
department stores (the original big-boxes); and with bare-
bones amenities, thanks to discounters. Discount stores became the leading retailers for children's clothes and toys; the
second largest segment for sporting goods, auto accessories,
garden products, housewares and domestics; and the third
largest outlet for health and beauty aids, jewelry, women's
clothing, shoes, and furniture.

A LITTLE RETAILER FROM ARKANSAS

In the early 1960s, Kurt Barnard had just become the founding director of the discounting industry's first trade group—the Mass Merchandising Research Foundation. One day, Barnard's secretary told him that a Mr. Sam Walton, who identified himself as a "little retailer from Arkansas," was there to see him in the trade group's Manhattan offices.

"Does he have an appointment?" Barnard asked.

"No, he doesn't," replied the secretary

"Tell him to go home and make an appointment like normal people. I'm up to my eyeballs here," said Barnard. "I can't see someone who just happens to come up off the street."

Barnard's secretary told him that Mr. Walton was very eager to meet him and to learn about the discount store business.

"I had in mind that he might become a new member," Barnard would later recall. "We badly needed members. I had eight or nine companies as members. That was clearly not enough. I told my secretary to tell him that I would see him for ten minutes, but only ten minutes."

In walked a short, wiry gentleman with a deep tan on his face and most improbably, a tennis racket under his arm.

"He graciously apologized and said he would only take ten minutes of my time," said Barnard, who today is president of Barnard's Retail Consulting Group. "Well, he stayed just a little over two hours. He asked pointed questions, and when I answered them, he jotted things down on a little pad that he had pulled out from his pocket. After those two hours, I realized I had been in the presence of one of the most remarkable men I would ever meet."[10]

Toys "R" Us: The Right Idea at the Right Time

As for Charles Lazarus, his timing could not have been more impeccable, thanks to a confluence of pivotal factors. The first factor was television—at the time, two-thirds of American TVs were owned by families with children under the age of twelve. TV was, of course, the ideal medium for advertising. Mr. Potato Head, which was invented and patented by a New Yorker named George Lerner, made its debut in 1952 as a prize for cereal premiums, and is generally acknowledged as the first toy to be advertised on television—initially a regional buy in California. Mr. Potato Head consisted of an assortment of plastic eyes, eyebrows, ears, a nose, a mouth, a hat, and a pipe, among other articles, which were designed to be stuck in a Styrofoam head (or a real potato) to make it look, well, human. Mr. Potato Head grossed $4 million (at the time, a very big number) in the first year it came out. In 1953, Mrs. Potato Head was introduced to the market. It wasn't until 1964 that the Potato Heads came with plastic bodies shaped (obviously) like potatoes. The Potato Head family gave birth to a new multibillion-dollar system of selling toys.

The second important factor was the arrival on the scene of the Mattel toy company, which was founded in 1945 in a garage workshop in Southern California by Ruth and Elliot Handler and Harold "Matt" Matson (who was eventually bought out by the Handlers). In 1955, Mattel began advertising its products on a new TV show for kids: Walt Disney's *Mickey Mouse Club* on ABC-TV. Mattel spent $500,000 (a huge amount of money at that time) to advertise the "Mickey Mouse Guitar," with a picture of America's favorite rodent on the front. Another big-selling toy was the air-powered pump action Burp Gun, which made a burping sound as it fired ping-pong type balls. The marriage of Mattel and Mickey revolutionized the way toys were marketed to children; parents wanted to buy toys they had seen advertised on television because those were the toys their kids were asking for.

"Pre-Mattel, there were no branded toys," said Bernard Loomis, a top executive at Mattel, and later president of Kenner Toys. "The business at that point in time was oriented toward a few major retailers, like Sears. Sears buyers ran the world. They picked an item here and an item there. The consumer wasn't looking for anything in particular. Then along came Mattel and the world changed. Mattel created a consumer-marketing business by creating a product that the consumer was looking for. A television-advertised toy became the number-one traffic builder in the most important season of the year."[11]

In 1959, Ruth Handler created a doll called Barbie (named after her daughter) that would eventually change the toy category from a seasonal to a year-round business. (At that time, the vast majority of all toys were sold by department stores during the six weeks before the holidays; the rest of the year, those stores sharply curtailed their stock.) Mattel later introduced Chatty Cathy, the world's first talking doll, which made it ideal for television advertising because young girls could see and hear the doll. It was such a runaway hit that some retailers sold the doll below cost in order to attract shoppers to their stores.

All of these developments helped Lazarus, who, in 1957, changed the name of his operation, because he felt that the words "Children's Supermart" were too long for his signs. Figuring that shorter words in bigger letters would be preferable to longer words in smaller letters, Lazarus came up with the most concise name he could think of and still convey what made his store special and unique: Toys "R" Us.

The first Toys "R" Us store consisted of more than eighteen thousand different toys stacked high in big (average size: ninety-three thousand square feet), bare-bones warehouse-type spaces. "There's an enormous opportunity in America if you're willing to make a commitment to inventory," said Lazarus, who could afford the huge amount of stocked goods because of the way the toy industry was set up: Retailers who ordered goods in the summer and received them in the fall didn't have to pay manufacturers until December or January. Because the prices were so much better than full retail, customers were more than willing to pull the merchandise from the shelves, pack them in their own bags and boxes, and place them in oversized shopping carts. "There was only our price and a very high price, so customers were willing to withstand a lot."[12]

According to Bernard Loomis, Toys "R" Us stores "weren't pretty; it was not important for them to be pretty. They had the merchandise; they had it where you could get at it. They tried hard to have enough registers so the lines weren't too long. Their reputation was that you could find what you were looking for and it would be at a good price."[13]

Lazarus instituted a no-questions-asked return policy because he learned early on in his career that, "the customer who raised his voice generally got his purchase taken back anyway, regardless of the merits."[14]

The store stocked products from all the major toy lines from manufacturers such as Hasbro, Mattel, Coleco Industries, Kenner Parker Toys, and Fisher-Price toys. Lazarus kept buying and kept stocking his stores with virtually everything a manufacturer had to offer. Having a showplace for their wares and a medium to advertise them, toy manufacturers aggressively added new products.

Prior to the advent of Toys "R" Us, the pattern of the retail toy business in the United States had changed very little for decades. Every February, the industry would gather in New York City for the Toy Fair trade show, where manufacturers would present their hot items for that year's holiday shopping season; buyers would place their orders for delivery in the summer, and pay for them in December or January. The new batch of merchandise was stocked in the stores around October. In the six-week period between Thanksgiving and Christmas/Hanukah, upward of 70 percent of all retail toy sales in American were rung up at the cash registers. By the mid-1970s, holiday toy sales accounted for about 50 percent of annual business. Today, new products are launched all through the year.

Lazarus committed Toys "R" Us to growth. By 1966, he had opened three additional stores. That year, he sold his four units for $7.5 million to a retail firm called Interstate Stores; as part of the deal, he stayed on to manage the operation. Over the next eight years, Toys "R" Us grew at an annual rate of 30 percent and, in the process, reached a total of forty-seven stores by 1974. That kind of growth was the sole bright spot for Interstate Stores. In 1974, citing problems with its discount stores, Interstate filed for bankruptcy. Deciding to concentrate strictly on the toy business, Interstate appointed Lazarus as chief executive officer. Four years later, the reorganized company emerged from bankruptcy as Toys "R" Us. In the immediate aftermath, the fortunes of Toys "R" Us were propped up by toy manufacturers, which granted the retailer liberal credit terms; after all, it was in their best interest to keep Toys "R" Us in business. Once it was back on solid footing, the category killer's annual revenues grew from $200 million in 1975 to more than $2 billion in 1985. Growth was boosted by the hot product of the moment, such as video games.

Centralized buying and computerized inventory management were essential to Lazarus's idea, and ultimately to every other category killer and big-box retailer. Every cash register in every store was connected to the merchandise-tracking system. If a store was running low on a particular toy, that data was transmitted to corporate headquarters (then in Rochelle Park, New Jersey), and the closest distribution system would replenish the item. Although Lazarus's formula was copied (unsuccessfully) by regional and national chains, Toys "R" Us was the category killer, forcing department stores and general merchandise discounters to either abandon the category or commit to running and keeping up a well-stocked toy department all year.

The influence of Toys "R" Us was felt in every corner of the business. For example, some manufacturers designed and sized their packaging so that it would fit on Toys "R" Us store shelves. More profoundly, Toys "R" Us often influenced *what* toys would be manufactured. Because of its enormous buying power, the retailer essentially held veto power over some products that didn't strike the fancy of its buyers. On the other hand, if a toy tested well at Toys "R" Us, manufacturers were emboldened to proceed with production. The company recast and then dominated the toy market by attracting shoppers who came to paw through toy inventories that were wider and deeper than they would ever find anywhere else, combined with low prices such as they had never seen before. That one-two punch could not be withstood by most traditional department store chains and mom-and-pop stores. Lazarus and his company shaved costs at every stop along the supply chain.

Sam Walton thought so highly of Lazarus that he named him to Wal-Mart's board of directors, on which he served from 1984 to 1989. "Walton was fascinated by Toys "R" Us and wanted the fifty-nine-year-old Lazarus on board so he could dissect him at leisure," wrote Bob Ortega in *In Sam We Trust*. Lazarus might never have suspected that Wal-Mart would one day sell more toys than his company; Ortega speculates that Walton certainly foresaw that day.[15]

The Toys "R" Us management understood that it had to expand its product assortment beyond the narrow toy category. History has shown that every subsequent category killer has had to do the same thing in order to stay competitive. Toys "R" Us added children's clothing and non-toy merchandise, such as disposable diapers, which they sold as a loss leader because customers who came to buy disposable diapers often stayed to buy toys. In 1983, the company opened Kids "R" Us, which offered a broad assortment of brand-name children's wear at competitive prices. Kids "R" Us ultimately became the biggest kids' clothing store chain in America, and drove out of business many mom-and-pop operations in that category. In 1996, the company went a little more upscale with Babies "R" Us, which featured specialized products that new parents must (or think they must) have, including apparel, furniture, car seats, bedding, and strollers. Babies "R" Us has emerged as the chain's biggest moneymaker, and now includes photo studios, baby care seminars and classes, free car-seat installation inspections, and assorted online services such as advice from noted authorities on child development.

The toy retailer has been one of the few U.S.-based category killers to successfully expand into international markets. The company opened its first stores outside the U.S. in 1984, in Singapore and Canada, and today has over 450 international stores (including franchise operations) in twenty-seven countries.

By deeply discounting his merchandise, Charles Lazarus began the trend of reducing once-expensive products to the status of affordable commodity goods, a trend that continues to this day. Reducing prices and putting most products within reach of the average consumer—this was the democratization of the consumer culture.

3

Category Killers Everywhere

Show me a thoroughly satisfied man—
and I will show you a failure.

—Thomas Edison

TOYS "R" US CREATED the template for category killers. The company presented to consumers big-box stores with an emphasis on self-service, big selection, low prices, and lots of parking. It conditioned baby boomers to a different kind of retail experience. The kid whose parents were buying toys at Toys "R" Us in the 1950s and 1960s eventually grew up to buy books at Barnes & Noble, power saws at Home Depot, printers at Staples, and pet food at Petco, and the shopping experience felt perfectly natural. Although the product categories were different, the approach was very much the same.

Bookselling

While Charles Lazarus was pioneering the category killer idea for toys, Leonard Riggio was studying engineering at night at New York University and working his way through school as a clerk in the college bookstore. Riggio, who came from a working-class background in Brooklyn, was hardly a man of letters. Admittedly not a voracious reader, Riggio considered book retailing "an elitist, standoffish institution" and has said, "If I got a job at a hardware store, I would have been Home Depot today."[1]

In 1965, after informing his boss that he could create a better student bookstore, the twenty-four-year-old Riggio put together $5,000 in savings and loans and did just that. He rented a small storefront on Waverly Place, just off Washington Square in Greenwich Village, and opened the Student Book Exchange, which became so successful that Riggio opened five more college stores.

Six years later, in 1971, Riggio borrowed $1.2 million to buy Barnes & Noble, a failing bookstore on Fifth Avenue and 18th Street, midway between the Empire State Building and Washington Square Park in Greenwich Village. The first Barnes & Noble store opened in New York in 1917; the Fifth Avenue store debuted in 1932. Riggio transformed the management team and expanded the inventory. He later added eighty thousand square feet of used books, remainders (out-of-print books), and best-sellers. Some of the out-of-print books were sold by the pound to customers pushing shopping carts. Twenty-five years before Jeff Bezos, founder of amazon.com, would utter the same words, Riggio dubbed his establishment the "World's Largest Bookstore."

But it wasn't just about size. Riggio wanted to transform the bookselling—and book-buying—experience. In 1974, he attracted new customers by discounting books—most notably the *New York Times* hardcover best-sellers—by 40 percent. Prices for paperback bestsellers were cut by 20 percent and all hardcovers by 10 percent, thereby altering the basic economics of bookselling.

In 1976, the Barnes & Noble Sales Annex superstore opened uptown at Rockefeller Center. Over the next decade, more Annexes were added around the Northeast. In 1987,

B&N acquired the B. Dalton Bookseller chain from the Dayton Hudson Corporation (parent company of Target Stores), to become the leading bookseller in the United States. Two years later, it added the Scribner's and Doubleday Bookshops chains. "The day I bought B. Dalton," said Riggio, "is the day I became a common enemy" to the other members of the small, clubby book world of writers, editors, publishers, and booksellers.[2]

The *horror* of it all was typified by a *Washington Post* article that decried a world in which, "Chain bookselling means best-selling books will be available everywhere, but it also means that they—and the tapes and the calendars—leave no room for the small-press edition of a minor novel or a university-press edition of an important scholarly work."[3]

Just to prove that the more things change, the more they stay the same, Macy's was faced with a similar backlash in 1909—yes, *1909*—when the retailer began selling books at 20 to 25 percent below the publisher's list price. A lawsuit filed by a book publishers association claimed that Macy's discounting practices had damaged the true value of their copyrights. Macy's countersued, charging that the publishers' group represented an illegal trust under the Sherman Antitrust Act. The only thing the publishers could do was to stop selling to Macy's, which responded by buying its book inventories from transshippers, wholesalers, other retailers who had overbought, and from the authors themselves.

In 1990, taking note of the Toys "R" Us big-box strategy, Riggio bought Bookstop/Bookstart, a Texas-based chain, which comprised twenty-four superstores in the southern and western United States. The following year, he began opening twenty-thousand-square-foot freestanding Barnes & Noble superstores. He has long argued that because each of his stores carries as many as ten times the number of books as a small store, he's actually increasing the choices for book buyers.

Riggio knew, of course, that a super bookstore could not be as frenetic and bare-bones as a Toys "R" Us. The idea was *not* to get people in and out quickly, but to give them reasons to stay. Long before Howard Schultz, the chairman of Starbucks Coffee, popularized the idea of a "Third Place" (home is the "First Place"; work is the "Second Place"), B&N created a locale with amenities such as public seating and restrooms, a place where people were encouraged to browse, to stay to buy another book . . . a magazine . . . some music; to relax in a comfortable armchair, nestled in a reading nook, while thumbing through a best-seller. Parents could sip lattes while junior was in the children's book section, entranced by a storyteller. Emulating the approach of smaller independent booksellers, B&N hosted community events, author readings and signings, and musical performances. In recent years, B&N has sponsored a summer reading program for kids. A child who can prove that he or she has read eight books since the end of the school year earns a free book. Being a part of the community is an ideal way to nurture young readers, who will grow up to become customers. Today, the company runs 652 Barnes & Nobles and two hundred B. Dalton Booksellers.

Less successful has been its Internet business, which remains an also-ran to Amazon.com and has never been profitable. In the fall of 1996, Leonard Riggio and his brother Stephen had a dinner meeting with Jeff Bezos and Tom Alberg, an Amazon.com director in Seattle, at which they explored the possibility of investing in the fledgling Internet retailer. Nothing ever came of those discussions, but if Bezos had been interested in selling all or part of Amazon.com to Riggio, it would have had a profound impact on the direction of Amazon.com in particular, and electronic commerce in general.[4]

IN 1971, brothers Tom and Louis Borders opened a small used bookstore called Borders Books on the campus of the University of Michigan in Ann Arbor. A former employee has said that the brothers dreamed of creating "a utopian bookstore," with a campus-inspired counterculture flavor that included hiring aging flower children, self-described political radicals, and well-educated idealists in Birkenstocks.[5] This "Utopia" was supported by the genius of Louis Borders, a gifted mathematician and a graduate of Massachusetts Institute of Technology, who designed a unique, sophisticated inventory-management system that could electronically follow the path of every volume from order to sale.

By 1988, Borders had expanded to four superstores. Eyeing an opportunity for national growth, the company brought in a new chief executive, Robert DiRomualdo, who had been at the helm of Hickory Farms. This was a prescient move by the brothers. Many entrepreneurial founders of category killers waited much longer before bringing in professional managers with experience in running large retail chains.

Four years later, Borders was acquired by Kmart Corporation, then owner of Waldenbooks (founded in 1962), which at the time was the only bookseller with operations in all fifty states, primarily in shopping malls. The Waldenbooks and Borders acquisitions were part of Kmart's diversification strategy in the 1980s and early 1990s, which also included Pay-Less Drug Stores, OfficeMax, and The Sports Authority. But in 1995, a year after it formed the Borders-Walden Group, cash-strapped Kmart, which was under pressure in its core Kmart stores business, spun off the book division in a public stock offering and renamed the new company Borders Group, with headquarters in Ann Arbor. Today, the Borders Group includes 436 Borders stores in the United States and twenty-three abroad, 750 Waldenbooks locations, and thirty-six Books Etc. stores in the United Kingdom. It has total revenues of more than $3.4 billion.

There are many who bemoan the dwindling numbers of independent booksellers who can hand-sell books to customers they know well—as opposed to the chains, whose buyers' job descriptions don't include interaction with customers. Membership in the American Booksellers Association, the trade group for independents, dropped from 5,132 in 1991 to about 1,850 today. In 1991, independents accounted for more 30 percent of all book sales; today that figure is under 20 percent.

Although many detest the super-booksellers and the online book retailers, those powerhouses are the reason that there are more books available in print today—approaching two million—than at any time in human history. Michael Korda, the famed editor in chief of Simon & Schuster, is a big booster of the big chains, declaring, "With the exception of the Carnegie libraries, nothing has ever brought literary culture to the hinterlands like the invention of the mall-based superstore."[6]

Home Improvement

Although The Home Depot was not the first home-improvement category killer (that honor goes to 84 Lumber, a chain started in 1956 by Joseph A. Hardy in Eighty-Four, a town near Pittsburgh, Pennsylvania), The Home Depot is now indisputably the dominant player.

In 1978, Bernard Marcus and Arthur Blank were fired from their executive positions at Handy Dan Home Improvement Center. Marcus, the son of a cabinetmaker who had emigrated from Russia to Newark, New Jersey, was a pharmacist by education and training. While working for the Handy Dan Home Improvement division of Daylin, Inc., he met Blank, a New York accountant working for Daylin's drugstore division.

Marcus was debating whether to sue Handy Dan over his firing when he ran into an old acquaintance, Sol Price, the founder of the Price Club member-warehouse retailer. Price, who was involved in a lawsuit of his own, talked Marcus out of suing because, he advised, a lawsuit would consume time and whatever money Marcus had left. Soon after, Marcus and Blank came across a 120,000-square-foot hardware store in Long Beach, California, called Homeco, which offered wide and deep inventory at discounted prices. Although the store was essentially bankrupt, Marcus and Blank saw great potential in the concept. They convinced Homeco's owner Pat Farah to join them in Atlanta, where they were about to establish what would become The Home Depot.

Their concept was to appeal to the do-it-yourself consumer with vast warehouse-like stores with concrete floors, where the lumber and hardware were stacked high on palettes, at low prices, and sold by knowledgeable, customer-service oriented employees. They wanted to create an authentic experience. As they described the operation in their book, *Built from Scratch*:

> *The idea for our stores was that they looked shopped. That is why we didn't originally put in a separate, rear entrance for the lumber buyers. It is why we had contractors and professionals go to the front registers, alongside the do-it-yourself customers. That creates action. We wanted the big stuff going out the front and loaded in the parking lots so that everyone saw it.*
>
> *On top of that, the do-it-yourselfers saw that the contractor buying two units of sheetrock paid the same price as they did. There was no secret back door or discount for contractors. We were priced right for everyone—not just a select group.[7]*

Buying directly from manufacturers enabled Marcus and Blank to offer dramatically lower prices that were supported by large sales volumes. The idea was for their competitors to "choke on our sawdust," as they wrote in *Built From Scratch*. Changing the whole concept of home-improvement retailing, they grew the company quickly and aggressively, adding stores in Georgia, Florida, Louisiana, Texas, and Alabama within the first five years.

In the early 1990s Charles Lazarus advised Marcus and Blank on how to reach their ambitious goals for expansion.

Lazarus said that when he was expanding Toys "R" Us, the most difficult thing he had to do was to "look at the people who have helped me build this company, get to a half a billion, then a billion and so on, and recognize that at some point along the way, they ran out of steam." Lazarus believed that recognizing that those same people "did not have the capacity to take me from a billion to $5 billion, from $5 billion to $10 billion" was his greatest challenge and would be their greatest challenge as well. Marcus and Blank concluded that an expansion-minded company can't "outgrow the ability of people to take you to the next level."[8]

During the 1990s, profits zoomed at an average annual rate of 35 percent. Home Depot became the world's largest home-improvement retailer, and the youngest retailer ever to break the $50 billion mark in annual sales. For seven years in a row, it was voted by *Fortune* magazine as "America's Most Admired Specialty Retailer."[9] In 2003, Home Depot had sales of more than $64 billion—of that amount, 35 percent had come from professional contractors.

The prototype of a Home Depot store is approximately 100,000 to 130,000 square feet with forty thousand to fifty thousand stock-keeping units of merchandise in eleven departments (lumber, building materials, flooring, paint, hardware, plumbing, electrical, lighting, garden, kitchen and bath, millwork, and decor). The newer stores usually include a 15,000- to 25,000-square-foot garden center. (This feature is not in its prototype urban stores, because few city dwellers have gardens of a significant size.) The stores offer a wide selection of services, such as in-store clinics to help customers do projects themselves, complimentary design and decorating consultation, truck and tool rental, home delivery, and free potting.

LOWE'S, THE OTHER major player in the home-improvement sector, has about a thousand stores (all in the United

States), more than half the number of Home Depot, and annual sales in 2003 of $30.8 billion. Three-quarters of Lowe's locations now are within ten miles of a Home Depot. Lowe's started out in 1946 as North Wilkesboro Hardware, in North Carolina, and was renamed Lowe's in the 1940s when H. C. Buchan bought out his partner and brother-in-law, James Lowe, and created a chain of small- and medium-sized hardware and building materials stores that sold to the trade as well as directly to consumers.

After a successful run of several decades, Lowe's was virtually on life support when it was resurrected in 1996 by Robert L. Tillman, a Lowe's employee since 1963. Tillman took an anti–Home Depot strategy. Rather than offering shoppers a warmed-over version of Home Depot's rough-hewn, steel-toed-work-boot, dusty-floor aesthetic, he redesigned and brightened up the stores to make them more appealing to women, who initiate the majority of home-improvement projects. (Home Depot would later take the same approach.) New stores were built larger (115,000 to 150,000 square feet) with wider aisles so that two shopping carts could easily pass each other. These stores, which were cleaner and neater, featured departments that were believed to attract women: lighting, accessories, paint, and flooring. Lowe's also added more appliances and high-end designer decorator lines.

Both Home Depot and Lowe's run free how-to clinics and workshops on home-improvement projects—from installing door locks to building a retaining wall—which create a sense of community among their customers and help to sell products. Home Depot earmarks the first Saturday of every month for a kids' workshop where young people, accompanied by a grown-up, learn how to build small projects, such as a memory box for precious possessions. Home Depot emphasizes this approach with its advertising tag line: "You can do it, we can help."

As retail consultant Paco Underhill has written, do-it-yourself stores "stripped hardware of its arcane side, rendering it unintimidating, even friendly, to the greenest tyro." Instead of merely hanging lighting fixtures on a rack or shelf, Home Depot and Lowe's display how the lights will appear and complement a room ensemble. Context has become important in interior decorating and display. This was accomplished by rethinking the stores' purpose as well as the merchandise they carried. Underhill further explains:

> *Stores that sold nuts and bolts gave way to stores that sold lifestyles. Under that vast umbrella, nuts and bolts and lumber and sheetrock could be sold alongside lighting fixtures and kitchen cabinets and Jacuzzis and frilly (and nonfrilly) curtains and everything else. These stores sold not hardware but homes. The retail hardware industry has gone from an "Erector set" mentality to a "let's play house" approach, from boys only to boys and girls playing together.[10]*

The combined sales of Home Depot and Lowe's now account for about 15 percent of the $500 billion home-improvement market.

Office Supplies

By 1985, Thomas Stemberg, a graduate of Harvard University and Harvard Business School, with a self-described "wild streak," had been fired from senior executive positions at two supermarket chains—Jewel's Star Market and First National Supermarkets, where he was president of the company's low-cost, high-volume Edwards-Finast division. Stemberg, the son of a restaurateur and caterer from Newark, New Jersey, is considered one of the people responsible for the development of generic supermarket products.

The way the story goes, on a Fourth of July weekend in 1985, Stemberg was unable to find a replacement ribbon for his printer in his hometown of West Hartford, Connecticut.

Both his neighborhood stationery store and the local computer store were closed for the holiday weekend. BJ's Wholesale Club was open, but didn't have the ribbon among its limited inventory of office supplies.

That's when Stemberg experienced his epiphany: Create an office-supply superstore with a cost structure that would ensure low prices. After studying the category, Stemberg concluded that most office-supply stores were too small to benefit from bulk buying, which would enable them to lower their prices. As a veteran of the supermarket business and a student of its buying and distribution efficiencies, Stemberg considered both Toys "R" Us and Home Depot essentially supermarkets for "bigger, bulkier goods." His aim was "to take the same approach and satisfy customers with lower prices." He drafted a business plan for a discount category-killer office-supply retailer, a "Toys "R" Us" type of operation, which would emulate Costco's strategy of offering discounted merchandise to small-business owners. After considering naming the company "8½ x 11," or "Office Mart," Stemberg eventually decided on Staples, The Office Superstore. "It had a nice ring to it (and the play on the word *staple* didn't hurt). We would provide the principal components for the office that works."[11]

Robert Nakasone, then a top manager at Toys "R" Us and later its chief executive officer, was a key adviser to Stemberg, who had known Nakasone when they worked together at Jewel Companies. "Smart and well versed in every detail of superstore retailing, Nakasone helped me build the conceptual framework of Staples and served as one of our first board members," Stemberg wrote. Another prominent director was Mitt Romney, then a venture capitalist with Bain Capital, who helped to fund Staples and who later became governor of Massachusetts.[12]

Staples opened for business in January 1986 in a five-thousand-square-foot space in an old mill building in Newton, Massachusetts (shades of the Ann & Hope discount operation!).

Four months later, the first store was opened in Brighton, Massachusetts, surrounded by many small- and medium-sized businesses. At first, Staples carried mostly stationery items—Post-it notes, printer ribbons (of course!), and paper products—because vendors of fax machines, copiers, printers, etc. were reluctant to sell them to the fledgling retailer, which would expand its selection to include adding machines, calculators, filing cabinets, and office furniture.[13]

It took just a few virtual minutes for a Staples competitor to materialize. In 1986, the same year that Staples debuted, so did Office Depot, Inc., based in Delray Beach, Florida, which opened its first store in Lauderdale Lakes, Florida. Two years later, OfficeMax opened its first store in the Cleveland suburb of Mayfield Heights. There were other rivals: Office World (partly owned by Montgomery Ward, in one of its last hurrahs), Office Club, Office Warehouse, and WORKplace, among others.

Today, Staples is the market leader, with annual sales of $11.6 billion, generated from more than 1,500 office superstores in North America and Europe (where it bought the mail-order business of French office-supply company Guilbert), as well as its Web site and catalogs. At the beginning of 2004, there were 1,100 Office Depot stores operating in thirteen countries, generating sales of more than $11.6 billion. A distant third is Office Max, which in 2003 was acquired by Boise Cascade for $1.15 billion in cash and stock. It has about a thousand stores, mainly in the United States, and sales of under $5 billion.

Growth will be the major challenge for office-supply superstores, as it is for all the category killers. As big as they are, Staples, Office Depot, and OfficeMax account for only 20 percent of the $285 billion office-supply market, and are being challenged by Costco and Sam's Club, which have successfully targeted the most profitable product categories, including computer paper and printer cartridges. Staples has found growth by emphasizing the delivery of office supplies to small businesses, a market that is also pursued by Costco and Sam's Club, which offer hypercompetitive pricing on a limited selection of basic products, such as printers, fax machines, paper, and CD-ROMs. Staples also reconfigured its product mix and trained clerks to be able to provide small-business owners with practical advice.

Pet Supplies

Like books and home improvements, pet products has two major players, PETsMART, based in Phoenix, Arizona; and PETCO in San Diego, California. Both offer a wide variety of products and services for pets. Together they account for about $4 billion in sales of small pets (excluding dogs and cats).

PETsMART, which was founded in 1987, operates more than six hundred superstores in the United States and Canada as well as a catalog and Web site. PETsMART Direct offers equine products through its State Line Tack catalogs and via statelinetack.com. PETCO, which was founded in 1965, also has more than six hundred stores (in forty-one states and the District of Columbia) as well as a catalog and Web site.

Like Home Depot and Lowe's, PETsMART and PETCO offer features that make them a part of the community. Both these category killers include salons where pets are bathed, cleaned, and groomed, from their paw nails to their teeth. They also offer pet training classes and full-service veterinary care. PETsMART holds a 38 percent equity position in Medical Management International, which operates Banfield, The Pet Hospital through hospitals and wellness clinics. Two-thirds of sales come from specialty products (such as Burberry pet carriers and beef-flavored toothpaste) and grooming services—rather than products such as premium, higher-priced dog food, which dominated sales a decade ago. This kind of highly specialized approach to the category lessens competition from Wal-Mart, which carries basic pet products. A mere forty of

PETCO's ten thousand products overlap with Wal-Mart's. Plus, Fido is allowed to accompany his owner into a PETsMART or PETCO store, which is not the case at Wal-Mart or Target.

Since early 2002, Robert F. Moran, former president of Toys "R" Us, Ltd., Canada, has been president and chief operating officer of PETsMART, which has as one of its directors Thomas Stemberg, founder of the Staples category killer.

Both PETsMART and Petco stores are a feast for the pet owner, with aisles and aisles of toys, food, treats, shampoos, beds, you name it, for virtually whatever pet you need, including magazines such as *Ferrets—The Ultimate Guide for Today's Ferret Owners*. Just as baby boomers sparked the growth of Toys "R" Us, aging pet-owner baby boomers with empty nests are doing the same for this category. Additional impetus comes from households with children ranging in age from five to seventeen. PETsMART and PETCO have succeeded by creating an emotional connection with their customers, and, along with the top discount stores, dramatically lowered prices for what was once a high-margin business dominated by supermarkets.

PETsMART eschews the term "category killer." According to spokesperson Lynne Adams, "We don't like the name because it conjures up an image of a large footprint, high ceiling, lots of product; not a lot of customer service. We think of ourselves as a specialty and destination retailer. We want to answer the customers' questions. They know we know what we're talking about. We know how they feel about their pets. We are in a business that's all about emotion. We are a place to come to show off your pet. Pets can shop in the stores. It's an emotional, rewarding experience for our customers."[14]

Although PETsMART was founded for the purpose of selling food and other pet-related products, it has evolved, in the company's view, into a tool to assist owners in providing total lifetime care for their pets. Adams explained that the stores were initially "built around how we managed our inventory and how we bought products. There was a consumables section (food, treats, and litter), hard goods (toys and leads), etc. That's not how our customer shops." PETsMART altered its inventory distribution system, which enabled it to open up the store layout and make it more consumer-friendly by designing the store around pet categories: a cat section, a dog section, etc. "We are designing our stores around how our consumers think, shop and live."[15]

Home Electronics

Both leading category killers in home entertainment began as small specialty stores. Circuit City's roots go back to 1949, when Samuel S. Wurtzel opened what was considered Richmond, Virginia's first retail television store—1,200 square feet of rented space in a tire store. Wurtzel dubbed his company Wards, which was an acronym for the names of his family members: Wurtzel, Alan, Ruth, David, and Sam. By the 1970s, under the leadership of Alan Wurtzel, the company was renamed Circuit City, selling brand-name consumer electronics, major appliances, personal computers, and music software. Sales in 2003 were $9.75 billion.

Best Buy was originally Sound of Music, an audio component systems retailer founded by Richard M. Schulze in Minneapolis. In the early 1980s, the retailer added video products and appliances and in 1983 renamed itself Best Buy. Today, Best Buy sells brand-name consumer electronics, personal computers, home entertainment products, car stereos, software, video game hardware, and accessories as well as major appliances, microwaves, vacuums, and housewares in more than six hundred stores and online. In store design, Best Buy is the more impressive of the two consumer-electronics category killers. The signage for each department is very clear and eye-catching, which makes Best Buy a very easy and convenient place to shop. Merchandise is arranged in departments identified as Entertainment Software, Digital Cameras and Camcorders, and Wireless and Satellite Systems. Sales in 2003 were $23.1 billion, giving the company a market share of 17.9 percent, compared with Circuit City's 9.0 percent, according to *This Week in Consumer Electronics*.[16]

Starbucks

Starbucks Coffee is, of course, not a "big-box" retailer, but it is certainly a category killer. What Starbucks lacks in the size of individual stores, it makes up for in sheer number—its eight-thousand–plus stores are ubiquitous in many cities.

Starbucks began in 1971, when three Seattle entrepreneurs opened a tiny store in Seattle's Pike Place Market, where they sold gourmet coffee beans. They named the shop after the first mate on Captain Ahab's ship *Pequod* from the Herman Melville novel *Moby Dick*. In 1981, Howard Schultz, who was then vice president and general manager of the housewares company Hammarplast, came to Seattle to find out about this little, four-store retailer that was outselling Macy's in a particular model of Hammarplast drip coffeemakers. Soon afterward, Schultz talked Starbucks's founders into hiring him as director of marketing and retail stores. Five years later, envisioning an American version of the coffeehouses of Italy, he led a group of investors to buy the company. (One of those investors was Jeffrey Brotman, chairman of Costco, who remains a director of Starbucks.) By the end of 1987, there were seventeen stores, a number that shot up to 165 in 1992, the year the company issued its initial public stock.

Starbucks has employed a simple expansion strategy of aggressively saturating an area with stores. It's not unusual for a new store to take some 30 percent of the business from another Starbucks in the neighborhood. This helps the company save costs on delivery and management and reduces customer lines at the separate stores while expanding customer traffic at all the stores in the neighborhood. This carpet-bombing strategy has brewed many jokes. An episode of *The Simpsons* once featured a shopping mall filled entirely by Starbucks stores; the satirical Web site, *The Onion*, ran this headline: "A New Starbucks Opens in Restroom of Existing Starbucks."[17] In the second Austin Powers movie, Dr. Evil has set up his offices in the Seattle Space Needle, which has been converted into a giant Starbucks. He is surrounded by baristas wearing the familiar Starbucks green aprons.

But there is a method to this madness. Starbucks would rather open new stores—which serve as their primary advertising and marketing tool—than spend the money on print or TV advertising. The stores essentially promote themselves.

The average Starbucks caffeine-head visits a store eighteen times a month, a rate of frequency unmatched in American retailing. Sales have climbed an average of 20 percent a year since the company went public, and same-store sales have increased between 6 and 8 eight percent every year, remarkably with a minuscule advertising and marketing budget of 1 percent of annual revenues, compared with most retailers, which spend an average of 10 percent. Unique among category killers, Starbucks, with annual sales of $10 billion, is not a product; it's a lifestyle. "We aren't in the coffee business, serving people," Schultz has said. "We are in the people business, serving coffee."[18]

Warehouse Clubs

"I guess I've stolen—I actually prefer the word 'borrowed'—as many ideas from Sol Price as from anybody else in the business," Sam Walton wrote in his autobiography.[19]

Sol Price—the same man who advised the founders of Home Depot—was a lawyer in the downtown San Diego firm of Procopa, Price, Cory & Schwartz. In the early 1950s, the New York native acquired an industrial warehouse property in downtown San Diego and began looking for a tenant. After some clients had taken Price to Los Angeles to check out a discount retailer named Fedco, Price decided that a discount warehouse retailer would be perfect for his San Diego property. In 1954, he and some partners launched FedMart, which targeted government employees, who paid an annual membership fee of $2. This initial venture was eventually expanded to a chain of forty-five stores. In the 1970s, controlling interest in the chain was acquired by a German company, which forced Price out and ultimately ran FedMart into the ground.

Undeterred, Sol Price, along with his son Robert, opened the aptly named Price Club chain in 1976. To keep their prices down, the Prices eschewed the expenses of advertising, credit cards, and deliveries in favor of limited hours, a highly edited selection of products, and a rapid turnover of those products that could be sold at the lowest possible mark-up. Borrowing from the E.J. Korvette playbook, Price Club customers paid an annual "membership" fee of $25. In return, they were able to buy brand-name merchandise at sharply discounted prices in large bare-bones warehouses with concrete floors and exposed steel girders. The idea was to sell television sets, canned goods, automobile tires, office equipment, and furniture displayed in cartons and on shipping pallets. Because margins were so small, the stores could be profitable only with high sales volumes and sixteen inventory turnovers a year—compared with four turns in a traditional store. The target market was entrepreneurs running small businesses. These customers were less concerned with the lack of amenities in the store than they were with getting the just-above-wholesale (9 to 12 percent off retail prices) deals.

In retail, the cliché "imitation is the sincerest form of flattery," certainly holds true. In April 1983, Sam Walton opened the first Sam's Wholesale Club in a suburb of Oklahoma City. Seven years later, there were 105 Sam's Clubs with annual sales over $5 billion. Clubs ranged from 100,000 to 135,000 square feet—about one and a half times the size of a typical Wal-Mart store.

Competition arrived six months later when the Costco Wholesale Corporation (originally called The Cost Company) opened in a former ship's chandlery in the industrial flats of South Seattle. Costco was the brainchild of Jeffrey Brotman, a Seattle attorney and businessman, whose father had been a successful apparel retailer in the Pacific Northwest. To lead Costco, Brotman recruited James Sinegal, who had first begun working for Sol Price in 1954 as a part-time checker at FedMart, while studying at San Diego State University. After working with Price for twenty-four years, Sinegal rose to the rank of executive vice president at Price Club.

The model concept for Costco was the European "hypermarket," pioneered by French-based Carrefour, which sold enormous quantities of food and general merchandise. Costco's strategy of selling fresh foods revolutionized the industry, and helped the organization grow from zero to $3 billion in revenues in an astonishing six years, a record. Price and Costco merged in 1993, at the same time that Wal-Mart acquired from Kmart ninety-nine PACE club stores and converted them to Sam's Clubs. Today, the two companies account for 85 percent of the wholesale-club market.

At first blush, their operations appear similar. They buy directly from suppliers and manufacturers, rather than from distributors (which helps keep prices down). Their warehouses comprise upward of 135,000 square feet (or the equivalent of two and a half football fields) and, combined with ample parking, can take up about fifteen acres of land, usually on industrial sites, which are less expensive than commercially zoned property. The floors are concrete (easy to clean) and are covered with pallets of products that are loaded onto steel racks by forklifts because less handling of merchandise translates to lower labor costs.

Warehouse clubs are shopped by "members" who pay an annual fee for the privilege. They are like old-fashioned variety stores on steroids, presenting a mélange of merchandise, including electronics, groceries, clothing, and hardware, at prices as close to wholesale as the average person is going to get. In some ways, they are the opposite of discounters in that they offer a pared-down, narrow, and deep selection of products. While the average supermarket offers customers thirty-five thousand stock-keeping units (SKUs) and the typical mass merchant presents 150,000 SKUs, the warehouse store stocks just four thousand or five thousand higher-priced branded SKUs in each product category. Costco effectively preselects the merchandise for the customer by, in essence, doing the comparison shopping and thereby telling the customer that it has negotiated the best possible deal at the best possible price in each category. Food and sundries account for about 60 percent of sales, ranging from staples such as name-brand electronics and clothing to seasonal merchandise such as golf clubs or skis. The chain also offers fresh meat sections, pharmacies, optical departments, and photo processing.

Costco sells to about one in every eleven people in the United States and Canada. One in four American households has a card-carrying Costco member. Its sales in 2003 were $41.6 billion, compared with Sam's $34 billion.

Costco always has been considered the more upscale of the two. Costco offers fine jewelry such as Raymond Weil and Baume & Mercier watches, and deeply discounted "treasure-hunt items" such as Waterford crystal and Coach handbags. Costco has become the largest retailer of fine wines in the United States, with sales exceeding half a billion dollars in a $20 billion industry, including retail and restaurant sales. It is one of the leading sellers of Veuve Clicquot Yellow Label Champagne and Dom Pérignon and is the nation's largest buyer of Bordeaux. The following joke, popular around Costco circles, illustrates the traditional difference between Costco and Sam's: A Costco shopper spots a display of Polo Ralph Lauren shirts, regularly retailing at $60, for $37. "I'll take four in white and one in blue," says the customer. A shopper sees the identical display at Sam's Club and declares, "I don't care how good a shirt it is, I'm not spending that much."

But that joke may represent the past more than the future. As Sam's Club has expanded to more affluent areas over the last couple of years, it has begun to take on Costco with its own upscale merchandise, including TechnoDiamond watches and cases of Courvoisier cognac, with labels taken from designs by Deco artist Erte, selling for $10,000.

NOW THAT WE'VE INTRODUCED the players and seen how they have gotten to their respective positions in the marketplace, we will look at the dynamics and the gestalt of category killers, and how they are influencing—and changing the face of—the retail landscape, both in the United States and abroad. The next four chapters will examine, respectively, pricing, competition, domestic growth, and international expansion of the category killers.

PART II

How and Why They Dominate

4

Pricing

The Cost of "Everyday Low Prices"

> While there was once a stigma attached with bargain
> hunting, the only thing consumers seem to be
> embarrassed about today is paying full price.
>
> **—Allen C. Questrom, chairman and
> chief executive officer, J.C. Penney Company**

THANKS TO CATEGORY KILLERS and discounters, we are living in the grand age of "everyday low prices" on virtually anything that's for sale. Back in the 1960s, pioneering discounters such as E.J. Korvette's catered to a small but significant segment of the population that was looking for a great deal. These shoppers didn't mind that discount stores were low on ambience—just as long as they were also low on prices. Today, virtually every shopper is looking for a great deal; in fact, in many cases, among today's shoppers there is greater allegiance to the *deal* than the dealer. They will comparison shop either in person or on the Internet until they find what they consider the best price. Consequently, a strategy of competing strictly on price is fruitless—because *everybody* has a low price, or close enough.

And these bargain-minded shoppers are not limited to the middle class. According to a 2004 survey by the American Affluence Research Center, the top eight retailers favored by the wealthiest (average annual income of $359,000) 10 percent of the U.S. population were (in order): Target, Home Depot, Costco, Nordstrom, Gap, Bed Bath & Beyond, and Best Buy.[1]

Several factors contribute to these low prices. Let's start with imported products made in low-wage countries, particularly China, which have exerted tremendous pressure on domestically manufactured goods. Many U.S. manufacturers have responded by moving their production offshore because, they say, that's the only way they can compete.

Wal-Mart, the largest single importer in the United States, and arguably the most efficient one, relies on China, particularly the southern region of that country, for cheap goods. China is attractive because of its abundance of inexpensive raw materials, cheap labor, up-to-date manufacturing facilities, modern infrastructure for moving goods via highways and ports, and a whatever-it-takes capitalist mind-set. Wal-Mart alone does business with more than three thousand supplier factories in China and, like other U.S. retailers, it is also involved in countries such as Bangladesh, Vietnam, and Honduras. Wal-Mart constantly pressures those manufacturers—and plays them off against each other—in a never-ending campaign to lower prices. While the manufacturers make a small profit, American consumers reap the financial savings when they buy inexpensive goods made offshore.

In addition, Wal-Mart has led the way in putting a lid on the price consumers pay, not only at Wal-Mart stores, but also at every other retailer as well. The prices found in Wal-Mart SuperCenters (150,000-square-foot stores that sell both general merchandise and groceries) are, on average, 14 percent below the prices of the competition, according to a 2002 study by UBS Warburg.[2] Wal-Mart is so powerful that it can slash prices on any item in any category at any time. For example, in the middle of October 2003, Wal-Mart caught Toys "R" Us and other toy retailers by surprise by slashing prices on more than a dozen hot-selling items, such as Mattel's Hot Wheels T-Wrecks playset. Several of those items were "loss leaders"—priced below cost in order to attract buyers. Nevertheless, Wal-Mart recorded profitable holiday toy sales in 2003, bolstered by solid gross margins. Less successful was KB Toys, with 1,231 outlets, most of them in malls, which declared bankruptcy.

The influence of the Behemoth from Bentonville on the price of goods is commonly referred to as the "Wal-Mart Effect," and it has exerted a tighter rein on inflation than a truckload of Alan Greenspans. By 2005, Wal-Mart will effectively save its customers some $25 billion, according to New England Consulting Group, which estimates that Wal-Mart's price-cutting influence on its competitors will bring about a combined annual savings for consumers of $125 billion.[3]

Today, Wal-Mart is the most powerful retailer in history. It has no rivals in sales of general merchandise and groceries. The combined sales of Target, Sears, Kmart, J.C. Penney, Safeway, and Kroger do not equal those of Wal-Mart which, at the end of 2003, had 1,555 Wal-Mart Stores, 1,397 SuperCenters, 525 Sam's Clubs, and 50 Wal-Mart Neighborhood Markets (a smaller store format) in the United States, and 1,293 stores in nine countries, generating combined annual sales of $253 billion. Nine cents out of every retail dollar spent in the United States ends up in the coffers of Wal-Mart, which attracts nineteen million shoppers daily.

The name of the game is efficiency. If you are not as adept as your competitor, and you must sell the same goods at a higher price, that's a recipe for failure. That's one simple reason why so many retailers—regardless of size and scope—go out of business. Scores of mom-and-pop stores close their doors every day because they are unable—or not creative enough—to compete with national chains that employ advanced techniques for information technology, inventory tracking, and logistics, and whose economies of scale make their operations so much more productive. Furthermore, because major retailers buy—and sell—in such large quantities, they are able to negotiate the best wholesale prices and pass the savings on to their customers.

Retail Pricing

According to *The Complete Dictionary of Buying and Merchandising*, "retail price" is defined as "the price a retailer puts on his goods for resale to consumers."[4]

Sounds simple enough.

Back in the old days, merchant retailers, who understood everything about their business, usually calculated the price of an item by figuring costs and multiplying by two—a process known as "keystoning." The merchant and/or his team usually relied on gut instinct to conclude when—and by how much—to mark down the merchandise in order to clear inventory.

Retailers could get away with this less-than-precise method when they had small operations. But when they expanded their stores into various regions, climates, and cultures, they had to be more accurate. Traditionally, in order to make the sale, suppliers would have to guarantee the retailer's profit margins through the payment of what is called "markdown" money, which enables the retailer to reduce the retail price of a slow-moving item, yet still emerge whole of out of the deal. The vendor pays that money to ensure its product's place in the store.

Today, retailers are required to have a thorough understanding of buying patterns and product movement—in real time. Retailers are employing new systems and technologies to figure out the most efficient and profitable ways of flowing their merchandise in their stores. New sophisticated, so-called "price optimization" software analyzes the buying patterns of customers to ascertain when to begin to mark down merchandise, and can make minute-by-minute price adjustments, including reacting to what competitors are selling the same item for. This is how the system works: Information analysts research their retail clients' databases to determine the past sales performance of products and the optimum inventory levels in stores and warehouses. Mathematical formulas and advanced algorithms (combined with variables such as weather conditions, seasonal buying patterns, and store locations) are used to forecast how and when consumers will purchase items, which are then priced accordingly. Every week, these analysts' programs transmit a new set of recommended markdowns to merchants and merchandise planners, who need only hit a button to adjust prices at the point of sale in their stores. Eventually, retailers will be employing electronically wired shelves and digital price labels that will enable them to instantaneously alter the price of an item and electronically transmit that new price to the computer screen on a customer's shopping cart; they will be able to offer the customer a special deal on an item that she frequently buys.

The Impact of the Internet

Led by Amazon.com and eBay, the Internet, which accounts for almost 5 percent (or more than $50 billion) of all annual retail sales, has had a profound influence on pricing. These two industry pioneers are the most visited multicategory commerce sites on the Web. Even retailers such as Best Buy, Circuit City, and Sears are using eBay as a way to generate profits by liquidating inventory—including overstocked merchandise, returned merchandise that might have cosmetic flaws, and discontinued models. It's a smart move because home electronics represents the second biggest sales category on eBay's site, following cars and car parts.

Amazon.com's presence in the physical retail world is most obvious in its relationship with Toys "R" Us, Borders,

Office Depot, Circuit City, and other brick-and-mortar retailers of various sizes and specializations. Amazon takes care of the Internet business for those companies; it also provides warehousing, order fulfillment, and site design. For example, when a customer orders a book from Borders.com (which is essentially a slight variation of the Amazon.com site—it is identified as "Borders teamed with Amazon.com."), Amazon bills the customer, ships the book, and invoices the sale; Borders earns a referral fee. The books are retrieved from Amazon.com's own inventory. The customer has the option of putting her book order on hold and then picking it up and paying for it at a Borders store. A link to BordersStores.com enables shoppers to search the Borders' inventory, where they can reserve a title for in-store pick-up at their nearest Borders store, which they can also find on the Web site. In turn, the partnership enables customers who order from Amazon.com to pick up their orders at Borders stores.

Amazon.com also oversees Toys "R" Us Web sites, including toysrus.com, babiesrus.com, and imaginarium.com (which sells educational toys). The various Toys "R" Us divisions are responsible for merchandising, planning, buying, and inventory management. Amazon.com manages the technology side, including Web site development, order fulfillment and customer service, and inventory in its U.S. distribution centers. At toysrus.com, customers are actually placing their orders into an Amazon.com shopping cart. A customer who wants to return a purchase online must return it to Amazon.com.

(The whole notion of in-store pick-up for online orders is becoming increasingly popular among shoppers who want the almost-instant gratification of getting the product the day they order it, and who don't want to pay shipping charges. About half of Circuit City's Web customers pick up their purchases themselves. Sometimes Circuit City will charge different prices online and in the stores. People who order online and pick up the item in the store, will be offered the lower price.)

In the spring of 2004, the Amazon.com–Toys "R" Us relationship hit the rocks when the toy retailer alleged in a lawsuit that Amazon.com violated an exclusive four-year-old agreement by allowing other third-party merchants to sell toys, games, and baby products on the Amazon Web site. Amazon then countersued, asking a superior court judge in New Jersey to terminate the partnership and award damages to Amazon. Amazon.com claimed that because Toysrus.com failed to select the most popular toys and baby products, Amazon.com was forced to offer its customers the opportunity to buy from other toy sellers. (At the time this book went to press, the dispute was not yet resolved.)

Thanks to the World Wide Web, consumers can easily research product specifications and comparison shop until they find the lowest price—as well as the most convenient retailer selling that particular item. Using online shopping services, consumers can make informed side-by-side analyses of brands, prices, features, and consumer ratings of merchants. Price-comparison technology has drawn the big hitters such as Yahoo! and Amazon.com, as well as smaller companies, most prominently Shopping.com, mySimon, BizRate, PriceGrabber, and Froogle, the shopping site of Google. These sites work best when comparing electronic products, which have obvious criteria, rather than, say, sweaters or dining room tables.

Search engines such as Google have become so important to electronic commerce that Amazon.com is developing its own Web-search technology because Web shoppers buy products through retailers they find by conducting Web searches, rather than by going directly to retailers' sites. Microsoft is improving its search technology and Yahoo! acquired Google's primary competitor, Overture Services Inc., on which retailers must bid for order of placement—the highest bid gets the top listing. By comparison, on Google, the search engine receives a fee from an advertiser only when a customer clicks on the ad.

Improved technology and wider bandwidth have further enhanced the online shopping experience. Christmas 2003 was appropriately dubbed the "first broadband Christmas" because of the proliferation of affordable, high-speed Internet access. The number of homes with broadband increased by 38 percent to twenty-two million, according to consulting firm IDC.[5] The greater data-transfer capacity of broadband makes it easier for shoppers to download visual images of products, which helps them comparison shop. Online shopping will only get bigger and bigger, but the stores will persist—we human beings still like to visit the marketplace, which is as much of a social and entertainment experience as it is a commercial transaction.

Controlling Inventory

In an era when customers just want more for less, category killers, discounters, and warehouse clubs must oblige by finding ways to drive down costs at every stage in the supply chain, because each stage adds to the cost of the item. Powerhouse retailers can compel suppliers to restock inventory only when necessary, so that the supplier—not the retailer—is paying for that inventory.

Electronic Data Interchange (EDI) enables manufacturers to control the production and flow of inventory along the supply chain to their retail accounts. Retailers, in turn, can track sales and transmit information to their distribution centers, which can plan the timing and amounts of product delivery to each individual store. The totality of this information is exchanged and shared over the Internet by both retailers and suppliers.

To further speed this real-time information tracking, eventually coming to an aisle near you will be products—everything from safety razors to cereal boxes—embedded with tiny microchips equipped with radio-frequency identification (RFID) that will enable these products to be scanned (like bar codes) and followed (via radio waves) by monitoring devices, from the factory shelf to the consumer's pantry. RFID information would then be sent to a central computer that would alert store personnel to replenish the store shelves and notify the vendor to ship more product. The result would be the biggest advancement in the concept of "just-in-time" inventory—delivery of the product just when it's needed, and not a moment sooner. RFID technology will free employees from manually scanning the bar codes of just-delivered merchandise. Although the technology is being employed in several industries, such as automobile manufacturing (to track components of a car), it has yet to make a significant impact in consumer packaged goods because the microchips, at present, are too expensive. The average cost of this type of RFID tag is about thirty cents; experts say the price must drop to a nickel before it becomes cost-efficient. New, special shelving will have to be installed in stores—another expense that will slow down, but not stop, the inevitability of RFID technology. Furthermore, consumer groups have expressed concern that information-rich RFID technology poses a threat to personal privacy.

It is not surprising the prime mover behind RFID—in its inevitable drive for greater efficiencies through technology—is Wal-Mart, which is more than a retailer; it's a technology powerhouse with the best information and logistics systems in retail. Its top 100 suppliers were charged to be ready to implement RFID by January 2005, and its next 200 suppliers to be ready by 2006. Other retailers involved in RFID include Germany's Metro Group, Tesco, Marks & Spencer, Prada, and Target.[6]

Self-Service: May You Help You?

Encouraging self-service among shoppers is another way that retailers are trying to keep down their prices while increasing their profit margins. In the mid-1990s, when unemployment was low and part-time workers were at a premium, Kmart and Kroger (the Cincinnati-based grocery store chain) began installing self-checkout stations, which allow customers to scan their own merchandise and then pay for the merchandise with a debit card, credit card, or cash. Checkout lanes—whether in supermarkets or home-improvement stores—are cost centers because retailers must have trained personnel in place to check customers out; there's no getting around it. That's one reason retailers encourage customers to use self-checkout lanes.

Although self-checkout machines ostensibly appeal to shoppers who want to quickly get out of the store, it is debatable whether the process is faster or more accurate than lanes with professional checkers. According to Greg Buzek, president of retail technology consulting group IHL in Franklin, Tennessee, "There is no question that, one-to-one, a staff checkout is faster than self-checkout. It's not perceived to be slower because there is usually nobody in line for the self-checkout, whereas there are people in line for the manned checkout. If you are the only person in line at both, the staff checkout will beat you every time because staff know how to use the system. In addition, there are security features built into the self-checkout device that cause a delay. You scan an item, you put it in a bag, and then you wait for it to be weighed. Normal checkout doesn't have to do that. The staff can scan two or three items in the time it take you to scan one on a self-checkout."

Interestingly, supermarkets that are using self-checkout lanes are finding that *shrinkage*—particularly employee pilferage—has been reduced, because, says Buzek, "Customers are more honest than the cashiers. A thief/customer is not going to wait to self-checkout to rip off the store because there is a camera, a scale, and other extra security measures."[7]

It is estimated that self-checkout systems, which cost about $80,000 apiece, can pay for themselves in less than a year and a half. After that, the savings in labor costs enables a retailer to cut the average cost of a transaction in half.

Since 2002, Home Depot has been a leader among category killers in using self-checkout lanes to get customers out of the store as quickly as possible, particularly during peak periods. Home Depot self-checkout terminals use computerized voices to guide customers—in both English and Spanish—through the process of scanning their items. A key to the system is identifying each item by weight through the item's UPC code. If there is a discrepancy between the item and its weight, the machine lets the customer know. If an item doesn't have a UPC barcode, the customer can press a button on the touch-screen monitor to find the product. The system stores the images and names of every product carried by Home Depot, down to enlarged images of every size of screw and bolt, and their codes.

Generally speaking, one store employee carrying a cordless scanner can supervise and monitor four electronic self-checkouts (which take up as much space as two or three stands with live checkers), be prepared to assist customers who need help, and watch for theft. Home Depot claims that cashiers armed with cordless scan guns can shave 8 percent off the average checkout time. So, for Home Depot, an added customer service is just as important as lowering the cost.

Another positive feature is that self-checkout lanes are not merely a device to cut the costs of labor; they can be a tool for optimally deploying labor for better customer service. By using self-checkout systems, stores can free up employees who had previously been working in the checkout area and reassign them to the sales floor to help customers. At a store like Home Depot, ideally, salespeople should be available to make sure customers find what they need, or to help out with advice or suggestions, let's say, in the plumbing department.

The "Commoditization" of Consumer Goods

The hypercompetitive consumer electronics category killers are not yet setting up self-checkout lines, but they are trying to find ways to stay profitable in a $100 billion industry that is besieged by Wal-Mart, Target, and Costco, as well a myriad of e-commerce sites and search engines that enable consumers to learn all about products features and to find the cheapest product prices. Because of these competitive pressures, specialty stores selling consumer electronics are battling in a world where even cutting-edge products can be sold at full price only for a short period of time. These products quickly become inexpensive commodity items—thanks to cheap imports from China and aggressive pricing from Wal-Mart, which recently replaced Circuit City as the number two electronics retailer behind Best Buy.

At his company's annual shareholders meeting in 2003, Alan McCollough, chairman and chief executive officer of Circuit City rhetorically asked: "Who would have thought that five years ago, when DVD was introduced at $600 (a player), that today the market share leader would be Wal-Mart? Because a DVD player is now $39 and you can throw it in a cart."[8] Consequently, in the face of the threat from the world's biggest retailer, the managements at Best Buy and Circuit City are rethinking their strategies. For that matter, when it comes to electronics, so is Wal-Mart.

Best Buy foresaw this "commoditization" of electronics products a decade ago when it became obvious that it no longer made sense to pay sales on commission in a world of such low-margin products as digital cameras and DVD players. Instead, Best Buy recognized that it must maintain its edge through customer service. Although they are not on commission, Best Buy employees are available throughout the store to answer questions about products, often in great detail. Product knowledge is essential when you're trying to sell big-ticket electronics products such as plasma television sets for upward of $3,000 or high-definition television sets costing as much as $10,000. These sales employees can explain the nuances of digital television technology and the variety of formats and technologies. To further enhance the shopping experience, Best Buy's stores are laid out in a very clear fashion. In addition, the company relocated its repair technicians from regional centers to in-store walk-up counters, which helps establish and maintain ongoing relationships with the customers. In 2002, Best Buy acquired a small Minneapolis-based computer-repair company called The Geek Squad. The technicians from The Geek Squad—all of whom wear black shoes, white socks, black slacks, white shirts, and black (clip-on) ties—are dispatched to customers' homes to provide such added-value services as in-home installation and repairs. The Squad has a national reputation for customer service, and has been featured many times in the national media and in books.

While Circuit City has also put an emphasis on in-home services, the retailer seems less sure of its path. Circuit City steadfastly maintained its commissioned sales force until 2003, when it converted six thousand commissioned salespeople to hourly wages, laid off 3,900, and hired additional "product specialists"—for a net loss of 1,800 sales employees—and closed most of the repair centers that supported its 626 stores. Circuit City is now 100 percent self-service, with customers taking the products off the shelves and putting them in shopping carts. To get better margins on private-label offerings, Circuit City turned to buying its products directly from factories in China.

Circuit City was considered the most credit-card dependent retailer in the United States. In fiscal 2003, credit income accounted for a jaw-dropping *100 percent of earnings*, according to Argus Research analyst Marie Driscoll.[9] By comparison, the percentage of profits derived from credit cards was 54 percent at Sears and 15 percent at Target. In 2003, Circuit City sold its bank-card business for $1.3 billion to Bank One Corp in order to concentrate on enhancing its retail business. Circuit City anticipates that its relationship with Bank One will generate annual pretax earnings between $27 million and $30 million. That's similar to the finance income it would generate if it retained the private-label finance operation.

CIRCUIT CITY'S MOVES are symptomatic of a big-box retailer that has been reduced to a product-delivery system that relies on sourcing, distribution, inventory flow, and getting customers in and out of its stores in the least possible amount of time. This type of system has encouraged consumers to demand low prices, which in turn, depress wages of workers. Today, almost one-third of working Americans now living in poverty are employed in the retail sector. The hourly wage for department store sales associates in 2002 was $8.79, according to the U.S. Department of Labor. The annual mean wage was $18,280. For clothing stores, the hourly mean wage was $8.45, with an annual mean wage of $17,750. In February 2004, the U.S. Department of Health and Human Services defined poverty level as $18,850 for a family of four. As consumers who demand everyday low prices, we are all partly responsible for these depressed wages.

Private Labels, Proprietary Brands, and Exclusives

With the increased number of retail outlets—physical stores, catalogs, Web sites—consumers have been given an abundance of choices as to where to spend their dollars. This enhanced retail capacity has had a negative effect on highly advertised national brands, which are offered almost everywhere at the proverbial everyday low prices. In the process, these brands have lost the power to help Store A differentiate itself from—and draw customers away from—Store B. This situation forces both Store A and Store B to find other ways to distinguish themselves.

Many category killers are responding by making substantial investments in their own private-label products. Private labels serve several purposes. First, these goods produce a greater profit margin because the retailers don't have to pay the built-in costs for the supplier's shipping, marketing, and advertising. With in-house brands, stores typically have no middleman vendor to pay, and they have more control over prices. By generating better profit margins, the retailer can afford to stock the national brands, which produce a thin profit margin. Second, a retailer can use a private label as a distinctive reason for shoppers to visit one of its stores. Third, the best retailers can market and merchandise their own private labels so well that the consumer believes them to be national brands.

A TRADITION OF PRIVATE LABELS

The private label has a long tradition in retailing. At Sears in the 1920s, company president Robert Wood was a firm believer in creating exclusive private-label products. The retailer's department of merchandise development created specifications for particular products and worked with manufacturers to produce those products at the best possible prices. The first of those proprietary items were automobile tires. After a national competition to select a name for the tire, a draftsman from North Dakota won with "Allstate"; the tire was introduced to the public in 1925. Six years later, Sears expanded Allstate into the auto insurance business. By the late 1970s, the profits from the Allstate business surpassed the profits from Sears' retail business.

In order to find a way to differentiate itself from its grocery competitors, Target's SuperTarget supercenters feature in-store Starbucks coffee shops, Einstein Bros bagels, Cinnabon, and the Cheesecake Factory. In its regular Target stores, the retailer carries a variety of proprietary lines including Mossimo Giannulli apparel; housewares from designer Michael Graves; Kitchen Essentials by Calphalon; and clothes, handbags, shoes, sunglasses, and jewelry from fashion designer/TV personality Isaac Mizrahi.

According to A.C. Nielsen, from 2001 to 2003, unit sales of store-brand goods increased 8.6 percent, compared with a 1.5 percent rise in national brands. Today, store brands account for 20 percent of all items sold at retail in the United States.[10]

In Europe, private label is much more important, particularly in Britain, where the penetration of supermarkets' own products is far higher in sales terms than anywhere else in the world. In the United Kingdom, own-label goods account for about 45 percent of super-market sales; in the United States, that figure is 20 percent. (One rea-son that private-label products are so popular in the United Kingdom has been its historical dearth of commercial television, which is one of the leading generators of brand recognition.) For Tesco, the lead-ing U.K supermarket chain, about 40 percent of sales come from its own brands, compared with 27 percent ten years ago.

Wal-Mart has been increasing its share of store brands—all of which, according to Wal-Mart strategy, must be the least expensive brands on its shelves. Wal-Mart reduces the prices for national brands in a wide variety of categories through its proprietary prod-ucts such as Ol' Roy Dog Food (named for Sam Walton's English Set-ter), which outsells Nestlé's Purina; Great Value bleach, which out-performs Clorox in some stores; and Alcott Ridge Vineyards, a line of wines produced by E&J Gallo. In apparel, Wal-Mart offers several proprietary lines, including No Boundaries, Faded Glory, and George.

Costco has been very successful with its in-house brand, which it calls Kirkland Signature, named after the leafy, waterfront Seattle suburb where the firm once had its headquarter offices. Kirkland Sig-nature brand products are intended to be on a par with the leading national brand, but at least 20 to 25 percent cheaper. Costco sells more than two hundred private-label items, including toilet paper, laundry detergent, cooking pots, and athletic shoes, accounting for about 11 percent of total sales.

Category killers are constantly searching for a brand-name product that can be sold at the lowest price. If they can't find it, they will work with a manufacturer to make a product under their own in-house brand. Costco does "co-branded" products with manufacturers, such as refrigerators and dishwashers by Whirlpool and jellybeans by Jelly Belly. One out of two ceiling fans sold in the United States is from Home Depot, and most of those are its Hampton Bay brand. The home improvements retailer sells 100 million gallons of paint annually; consequently, it has enough buying power to compel paint companies to alter their palettes for the year. In 2002, Home Depot worked with Disney to produce a new line of paint that was targeted at children. (Part of the sell was that color-sample chips came with mouse ears.) John Deere makes a line of lawn tractors for Home Depot that sells for a quarter of the price of Deere's introductory models. Rival Lowe's persuaded Troybilt to do the same.

What sets this generation's private-label approach apart from past behaviors is that customers who are loyal to a particular retailer are in many cases demonstrating greater trust in—and loyalty to—that retailer's private-label products. In effect, retailers have become managers of their own brands, which stand for more than a lower price. These private-label goods can match the most famous branded goods in quality and performance.

The toy category is an exception. One of the problems that Toys "R" Us has historically faced is that many of the brand-name products from Hasbro, Mattel, et al. it carries can also be found at Wal-Mart and Target—and often at a cheaper price. To try to remedy that situation, John Eyler, the CEO of Toys "R" Us, has greatly increased his company's supply of exclusive and private-label products, including vehicles, sporting goods, dolls., G.I. Joe action figures, and Animal Alley plush animals (which alone bring in more than

$200 million worldwide). In 1999, exclusive toys comprised only 5 percent of the Toys "R" Us inventory; in 2004, that figure jumped to about 20 percent. Eyler has said publicly that on exclusive products, his company earns margins that are between 15 and 20 percent higher than the more widely available branded goods.

Toys "R" Us has also started to offer a line of kids' play tools and real tools that are developed and packaged under the Home Depot label. And in 2003, in an interesting bit of synergy, Toys "R" Us began a relationship with the Albertsons supermarket chain, which set up Toy Box shops in many of its 2,300 food and drug stores, including its Jewel-Osco, Max Foods, and Sav-on Drugs divisions. The store-within-a-store concept—ranging in area from two hundred to five hundred square feet—offers unbranded toys selling for $25 and under—an ideal last-minute gift stop for grocery shoppers remembering that they need to get something for their niece or nephew's birthday. The Albertsons distribution channel is an opportunity for Toys "R" Us to sell products throughout the year with a retail partner that generates significant customer traffic. Toys "R" Us has a similar arrangement with the Royal Ahold supermarket chain in the United Kingdom.

On another front, to combat Wal-Mart's cheap prices, Toys "R" Us has been using its specialty-store ambience to entertain kids. Camp Geoffrey, named after the chain's giraffe mascot, consists of a free afternoon in-store activity, held three days a week for six weeks each summer. Although the "camp" is scheduled for two hours, most small children last for only a few minutes before getting a tour of the store, and a good look at all the things that they must have. Toys "R" Us claims that one million young "guests" attended Camp Geoffrey in 2003. Activities are built around popular products. As Toys chief marketing officer Warren Kornblum said: "In a world with Wal-Mart, Target, and those sorts of strong competitors, we believe that for us to succeed, we need to have a relationship with moms and not make toys just a commodity purchase."[11]

In 2002, Best Buy, which sells almost 10 percent of all the consumer personal computers in North America, (trailing only Dell) began selling its own in-house desktop brand, VPR Matrix. It was a logical move for Best Buy, where PC sales comprised almost 10 percent of its $21 billion in sales in fiscal 2003. PCs manufactured by the likes of Hewlett-Packard and its Compaq division have become commodities, with low margins. By comparison, the VPR Matrix, designed by Porsche Design GmbH of Austria (the studio that designed the car of the same name) has a distinctive look, including a brushed-metal casing, and comes with lots of cool features and high-end components, which makes it stand out. Best Buy later added a VPR Matrix laptop.

Barnes & Noble has been involved in self-publishing since the mid-1970s. After getting numerous requests for out-of-print books, the company acquired reprint rights for a variety of academic and esoteric titles and sold them for $6.99 apiece. In the 1980s, B&N expanded its publishing projects to richly illustrated coffee-table books on gardening, cooking, and lifestyle. In 2002, B&N bought Sterling Publishing Company, Inc., a Manhattan-based specialist in how-to and crafts books on everything from chess to gardening. The acquisition gave the bookseller a potent national sales force and distribution system that enabled the titles to be sold in rival book stores, as well as gift shops and a wide variety of specialty retailers. B&N's decision to buy Sterling didn't sit well with competitors; Borders and Costco announced that they would no longer carry Sterling titles.

In 2003, B&N reworked its series of Barnes & Noble Classics with the launch of fifteen titles, including *Huckleberry Finn*, *Middlemarch*, *Moby Dick*, *The Odyssey*, *Dracula*, *The Red Badge of Courage*, *Great Expectations*, *Jane Eyre*, *The Scarlet Letter*, and *The*

Souls of Black Folk, in a variety of formats, including hardcover, trade paperback, mass-market paperback, and eBooks, ranging in price from $3.95 to $9.95. This is an interesting strategy in a category where content and price supersede brand name. Because Barnes & Noble doesn't have to pay the 50 percent markup that a publisher would normally get, the lower-priced self-published books become more profitable. This puts B&N editions in direct competition with classics published by Modern Library, an imprint of Bertelsmann AG's Random House Inc. and Pearson PLC's Penguin Classics imprint. But B&N's books will have the advantage of being featured throughout its nine hundred stores, displayed with special signs and fixtures.

The bookseller also offers tomes on astrology, food, wine, and popular culture, and co-publishes *TV Guide Film and Video Companion*, *Encyclopedia Britannica Almanac*, the *MapQuest Road Atlas*, and, in a joint venture with Warner Books, *Satisfaction: The Art of the Female Orgasm*, by Kim Cattrall, star of the HBO television series "Sex and the City," and Mark Levinson. In the summer of 2002, Barnes & Noble dropped the CliffsNotes study guides, published by John Wiley & Sons, and replaced them with its own SparkNotes, priced at a dollar less than CliffsNotes.

By the end of the decade, B&N projects its own titles will comprise 10 to 12 percent of its total revenue by 2008, up from 4 percent in 2004. This is part of a crucial strategy in an industry in which new book sales grew only 1.3 percent from 1997 to 2002, according to the Book Industry Study Group.[12]

Another reason that Barnes & Noble was compelled to expand into private-label publishing was the demand of book buyers for lower prices, which they can get—particularly on bestsellers—from nontraditional booksellers such as Wal-Mart, Target, and Costco. (Ironically, it was Barnes & Noble that pioneered the idea of aggressively discounting best-selling titles as a way to attract customers.) In 2002, some $450 million was spent on general-interest books at mass-merchandise retailers, according to Ipsos Book Trends, up 7.4 percent from 2000. Such books now account for 30 percent of all general trade book sales.[13]

Because they are capable of moving tens of thousands of copies of books a week, the big-box stores have shaken up the publishing industry. Pennie Clark Ianniciello buys books for Costco and is such an important player in book publishing that the *Wall Street Journal* ran a front-page feature story on her power and influence. Publishers seek out—and follow—her advice on cover designs and marketing plans. Her monthly "Pennie's Pick," which is sent out to millions of Costco customers, is almost as good as a recommendation from Oprah Winfrey.

The warehouse clubs and discounters—which sell primarily popular fiction, cookbooks, how-to books, and children's books—treat the printed word just as they would toilet paper or AAA batteries. They buy a relatively few titles—two hundred compared with Barnes & Noble's two hundred thousand—and keep them on the shelves for about six weeks, then send them back to the publisher if the books aren't moving.

Brand Extension

When it comes to extending an established brand to other products, no category killer does it better than Starbucks Coffee, which is constantly finding ways to leverage its brand into other product categories and channels of distribution. In 1995, the company launched Starbucks Ice Cream with the Dreyers Grand Ice Cream company; sold primarily through supermarkets and grocery stores, it became the best-selling coffee ice cream in the United States. The following year Starbucks entered into a joint venture with PepsiCo. Inc. to develop a bottled ready-to-drink version of Starbucks' Frappuccino coffee beverage. Today, Starbucks bottled Frappuccino and Starbucks

DoubleShot command almost 90 percent of the U.S. ready-to-drink coffee market. There are currently seven Frappuccino flavors, which are sold in supermarkets. Starbucks also owns the Tazo line of premium teas.

In 2004, Starbucks teamed up with the Jim Beam unit of Fortune Brands to develop a premium coffee liqueur to be sold in bars, restaurants, and liquor stores, not Starbucks stores. This effort represents Starbucks' first attempt to tap into the alcohol business.

Over the past few years, the chain has become a small, but significant purveyor of the kind of music enjoyed by its core group of twenty-five-to-forty-year-old patrons. Starbucks sells its own compilation disks of CDs through Hear Music, a four-store San Francisco-based boutique music retailer that Starbucks acquired in 1999. The CDs are sold at most Starbucks stores in the United States. By the end of 2003, Starbucks had released a hundred albums and sold about five million CDs, including the Artist Choice series, in which performers like the Rolling Stones and Ray Charles pick their favorite tracks by other artists.

Since the middle of 2002, Starbucks has teamed with T-Mobile to create what some say is the world's largest Wi-Fi (wireless fidelity) network, which allows customers with laptops and handheld computers equipped with Wi-Fi cards to wirelessly access the Internet at speeds up to fifty times faster than a dial-up connection, for a subscription of about $30 a month. Patrons can check their e-mail, surf the Web, or download multimedia presentations available through Starbucks, such as film footage of blues musicians like Howlin' Wolf and Muddy Waters. On average, 70 percent of Starbucks customers stay in a store five minutes or less, with the other 30 percent spending about twenty minutes. But Wi-Fi users stay an average of forty-five minutes.

In 2004, Starbucks partnered with Hewlett-Packard to enable customers to listen to music downloads from twenty thousand albums using HP tablet PCs and then burn their own customized CDs at Starbucks stores. This program will transform the digital music at retail. Starbucks, which acquired licenses for the tracks, charges $6.99 for five songs and one dollar for each additional song.

Starbucks also has had great initial success with its Duetto Visa Card—the first prepaid cash card to double as a charge card—which was launched in fall 2003. The product of a partnership between Starbucks, Bank One, and Visa USA, the Duetto combines a Starbucks prepaid debit card with a Visa charge card that customers can use for purchases at Starbucks and other retailers. For each dollar they charge, cardholders earn a penny on their Starbucks account. This money— Duetto Dollars—can be redeemed for Starbucks coffee products or other merchandise. Cardholders also have the option of contributing a portion of their account to charity. More than twenty million Starbucks customers own the reloadable cash cards, which comprise 20 percent of the sales.

Category Management

For the past couple of years, the term "category management" has entered the retail lexicon in virtually every merchandise category. Category management began in the supermarket business, where big retailers of packaged goods learned that they could improve sales and profits if they could more efficiently administer all their different product classifications. The idea was to oversee the store not as aggregation of products, but rather as an amalgam of categories, with each category unique in how it is priced and how it is expected to perform over time.

One vendor is designated as "category captain" and charged with helping the retailer define the category; determine its place within the store; evaluate its performance by setting goals; identify the target consumer; divine the best way to merchandise, stock, and display the category; and then influence the implementation of the plan. Becoming a captain is obviously an important position because it offers that supplier an opportunity to sway a retailer's buying decisions.

Sure, you say, category management would work with pet food or shaving cream or lawn furniture, but certainly not *books*. Gregory Josefowicz, the chairman and chief executive officer of the Borders Group, the parent company of Borders Books & Music, begs to differ with you. As a teenager in the 1980s, Josefowicz started his career in the supermarket business as a grocery bagger at what eventually became the Jewel-Osco Division of the Albertsons chain of food-and-drug stores. That's where he absorbed the lessons of category management. Twenty-two years later, he became president of Jewel-Osco before resigning in 1999 to join Borders.

In 2002, Josefowicz brought category management to Borders. Publishers were selected to co-manage some 250 categories in their special area—cookbooks, business, children's, computer, how-to, sports, etc.—to identify the titles that the store would stock, how many of those titles would be in each store; even how they would be displayed, grouped together, placed in the store, allocated space, and so on. Category managers pay about $110,000 annually to help defray the initial costs of marketing research associated with the program.

What's in it for publishers? A seat at the table at which the major decisions are being made. While category managers can't pick all of their titles, they have the opportunity to shape a department. Borders insists that it has the final say over the titles it carries and that all publishers will share the benefits of the market research.

As you can imagine, this approach did not sit well with some members of the literary community. In the summer of 2002, Ralph Nader, Noam Chomsky, and twenty-six other prominent authors, signed a letter to Josefowicz, arguing that category management would hurt small publishers and narrow the stores' selection. "There is a difference between books and Pop-Tarts," the letter warned. "Leave the category management to the soap merchants."[14]

But the defenders and stakeholders of category killers and other big-box retailers will tell you that they must closely manage their costs and their prices by whatever means necessary. As consumer products continue to become low-priced commodities, as savvy consumers easily comparison-shop prices on the Internet, and as profit margins become thinner, only the smartest retailers, employing the best systems and technologies, will be able to survive. Everyone along the line pays for the costs of "everyday low prices."

5

Competition

There Used to Be a Department Store Here

Consumers are statistics. Customers are people.

—**Stanley Marcus, Chairman Emeritus, Neiman Marcus**

AT THIS POINT, we will examine how category killers contributed to the steady and inexorable shrinking of the department store business. While category killers have been a major factor in this decline, they are not as large a factor as the department stores themselves, who abandoned categories and opened the way for category killers to cherry-pick sectors of their business.

The Ascendancy of Department Stores

Once upon a time, department stores were the disruptive force in retail because they filled a void in the marketplace. One could say that department stores were the original big-box stores—comprising several hundred thousand square feet of space, the classic downtown department store dwarfs even the largest warehouse club store.

Back in the early days, U.S. retailing was composed of a disorganized collection of general variety stores and specialty shops that were the lifeblood of the community. These retail establishments were complemented by peripatetic peddlers, who traveled with their merchandise through rural America on foot, on horseback, or by wagon. Urban areas offered more sophisticated specialty shops and a greater variety of peddlers and street vendors, who often sold their wares at temporary outdoor spaces. The inefficiency of this system of distribution of goods created an opportunity for enterprising minds to create a new concept of selling: the department store.

If Bon Marché in Paris was not the world's first department store, it was certainly the most famous and influential. Originally a small piece-goods store founded in 1838, Bon Marché expanded under owner and founder Aristide Boucicaut, who went against conventional wisdom by continually adding new categories of merchandise—women's coats and dresses, shoes, etc. (At one time, the state had even banned the selling of more than one category.) Boucicaut sustained the sizzle of his store with customer service features, such as free home delivery to Paris residents, and free delivery for all catalog purchases of more than twenty-four francs. More than 150 years later, Jeffrey Bezos of Amazon.com boosted sales through free shipping on orders over a certain amount and many analysts thought he was a genius. Everything old is new again.

In the United States, in 1848, Alexander Turney Stewart, an immigrant from Northern Ireland, opened the nation's first department store in lower Manhattan, which he dubbed the Marble Dry Goods Palace. Fifteen years later, he expanded to a larger store on 2.5 acres on lower Broadway. Ballyhooed as "The Greatest Store in the World," the eight-floor Cast Iron Palace featured live organ music, predating Nordstrom's signature in-store piano player by more than century.

The period from 1860 to 1910 saw the rise of general merchandise dry goods stores, which ultimately became department stores. Responding to the increase in population of the cities, hundreds of department stores popped up all across the country, including many that would become famous names such as Rich's in Atlanta; Hudson's in Detroit; Dayton's in Minneapolis; Lazarus in Columbus, Ohio; Zions Cooperative Mercantile Institution in Salt Lake City; and Frederick & Nelson in Seattle. But department stores were not universally embraced. A Philadelphia newspaper editorialized against the department store for "going beyond its proper province." Clergymen damned them from the pulpit. Small shopkeepers charged that the "Department Store Octopus was consuming them." A small store advertised: "It is better to have 1,000 storekeepers fairly prosperous than two or three millionaires and 997 bankrupt tradesmen."[1] These arguments anticipate today's debates about the dominance of big-box category killers.

Department stores succeeded because they provided middle-class urban shoppers with a convenient place to buy a wide selection of superior goods at affordable prices, under one roof, in buildings noted for their inviting ambience, ornate architecture, grand scope, and sharp and courteous customer service. By definition, these stores had virtually everything. They were the forerunners of the shopping mall because they offered customers a one-stop, everything-under-one-roof shopping experience, particularly for the so-called "carriage trade" (a name that dates back to the time when wealthy patrons arrived via carriage. They were a destination in the heart of downtown, with something for every member of the family.

The New Shopping Destinations

After World War II, a newly prosperous American population began moving out to the suburbs, and retailers soon followed them with shopping centers. There eventually would develop three types of centers:

- A neighborhood center anchored by a supermarket

- A larger community center anchored by a discount department store

- A still-larger regional center anchored by department stores

The regional centers offered lots of space, free parking, expanded shopping hours, and, often, an edited version of what could be bought at the big downtown "flagship" store. Although the flagships still retained their majesty and distinction because they were much bigger and more elaborate than their suburban outlets, their dominance peaked by the late 1950s, when they became of secondary importance to the branch stores, which were smaller and more conducive to cohabitation with small, specialty suburban retailers. The size and scope of the downtown flagships were a testament and a monument to another time. No one ever did—or ever will again—build a store that big (several hundred thousand square feet) in the middle of a big city.

"PALED WITH DESIRE":
THE CREATION OF THE DEPARTMENT STORE

Aristide Boucicaut, the son of a successful hatmaker, and his friend and partner, Paul Videau, opened the Bon Marché department store in 1838 on the rue du Bac, in the Saint-Germain district of Paris. Over the next seventeen years, Boucicaut, who had worked in a large dry goods store on the same street, gradually expanded his merchandise offerings at Bon Marché (which translates to "good deal"), eventually moving to a new, larger location. He lured shoppers by selling many different types of goods under the same roof. The innovative Boucicaut allowed people to come into the store and browse without having to buy anything. He preferred taking a small mark-up on fast-moving inventory rather than taking a big mark-up on slower-moving items. He established fixed, clearly marked prices on everything he sold and instituted a money-back guarantee on all purchases. Whether he invented all these practices is open to question, but Boucicaut was definitely a retailing showman. He captured the romance of shopping for the chic French female of the day while creating, in his own words, "a cathedral of commerce, for a congregation of customers"—ladies of leisure, who had the time, the patience and the money to luxuriate in the sensual pleasures of commercial opulence.[2]

The novelist Emile Zola based his novel *Au Bonheur des Dames* or *The Ladies' Paradise* on Bon Marché, where he would spend hours on research, observing the acquisitive customers, who inspired him to describe scenes such as the following: "Women *paled with desire* [emphasis mine] and leaned over as if to see themselves, secretly fearing they would be captivated by such overwhelming luxury and unable to resist the longing to throw themselves in and be lost in it." In his novel, Zola described the fictionalized version of Bon Marché as "a riot of color, a street full of joy, a large open area devoted to consumerism where everyone could go and feast their eyes."[3]

Boucicaut depicted the necessary ingredients to create such an atmosphere—in real life:

> *What's necessary . . . is that they walk around for hours, that they get lost. First of all, they will seem more numerous. Secondly . . . the store will seem larger to them. And lastly, it would really be too much if, as they wander around in this organized disorder, lost, driven, crazy, they don't set foot in some departments*

*where they had no intention of going, and if they don't succumb
at the sight of things which grab them on the way.*[4]

In the United States, when department store pioneer A. T. Stewart began running the Marble Dry Goods Palace, few if any U.S. retailers posted a fixed price for their merchandise. Merchants charged whatever price the customer would pay, and because few of them stood behind what they sold, *caveat emptor* (let the buyer beware) was the order of the day. Shoppers could haggle with merchants and clerks as if they were at a street bazaar. Because an affluent-looking customer might be charged a higher price than a less affluent-looking one, some shoppers purposely dressed down in tattered clothes in order to be quoted a lower price—all subject to negotiation, of course.

Stewart believed that all this dickering was a waste of time and energy for both his clerks and customers. More important, the practice discouraged customer loyalty. Stewart became the first retailer in New York to institute posted, fixed prices, which appeared in newspaper advertisements and in the store. Although Stewart's move was initially dismissed by rivals as a gimmick, these competitors soon followed suit.

In Chicago, Marshall Field took back and refunded the full price of any item bought in his store. "The best way to show a lady that the merchandise she purchased is worth the dollar she paid for it is to give her the dollar in return," said Field, who immortalized the slogan, "Give the lady what she wants." And in Philadelphia, the innovative John Wanamaker created the first in-store restaurant and the first installation of the pneumatic tube, which sent money in little tubes traveling by air compression to another location in the building where change could be made.

The department store was the vehicle for the allowed middle-class urban shoppers to buy superior goods at affordable prices, thanks to the stores' buying power, fixed-price policy, and money-back guarantees.

Although the postwar period is often considered the beginning of the era of suburban shopping centers, its history runs much deeper. Country Club Plaza, a forty-acre site five miles south of Kansas City, Missouri, was designed in 1922 as the first suburban shopping district in America. To complement a residential community that he helped develop, entrepreneur Jesse Clyde Nichols created a space noted for its Spanish architecture—fountains, murals, courtyards, and stucco buildings with red tile roofs and ornate towers amidst streets and sidewalks. Initially, Country Club Plaza was populated by small, independent shops; neither chain stores nor branches of downtown department stores were allowed. It took seven more years before the next bold retailer, the Strawbridge & Clothier department store, built a branch store at Suburban Square, in the Philadelphia suburb of Ardmore, in 1930.

Eventually, department stores and their development arms led the way in constructing shopper centers in the suburbs. The idea behind the regional and super-regional centers was to replicate the kind of shopping and services that were previously available in small towns, but offer larger selections and easier parking. By 1976, three-quarters of all department sales in the United States were recorded in branch stores. When it came to shopping, the suburbs were king.

"Everything we did we copied from downtown—how many jewelers, how many women's wear shops," James B. Douglas, then president of the Northgate Company, the corporate developer of the Northgate Mall in Seattle, said in an interview in *America's Marketplace*. "I'd go downtown and study the trade that was in-between the department stores."[5] Douglas measured the linear footage of the various storefronts to calculate how much space to designate for each retail category within Northgate. When it opened on April 21, 1950, Northgate became one of the first regional shopping centers defined as a "mall." (The word was derived from the British game of pall-mall, or "ball and mallet," which included components of golf and croquet and was played on a fairway green.) With Bon Marché as the anchor of the mall, the Northgate design became the prototype of the shopping mall.

Similar moves were being replicated all over the United States. In the early 1950s, Leonard Farber, the first president of the International Council of Shopping Centers, the industry trade group, said, "the demand for shopping centers was so great, a developer could pick his site simply by using a map of the United States as a dartboard."[6]

The shopping center industry grew from 940 centers in 1957 to some 2,000 three years later. By 1977, there were almost 20,000 centers, and in 2004 there were more than 46,000 (including 1,150 enclosed malls), according to the International Council of Shopping Centers. These malls attract almost 200 million adults every month. Of course, as they grew, shopping centers attracted their share of critics, who disliked their hermetically sealed sameness, their dedication to consumption, their size and scope, and their part in devastating the retail corridors of small downtowns. The renowned architect Cesar Pelli, who once designed shopping centers and later served as the dean of the Yale University School of Architecture, said in the 1970s, "Malls succeeded because they approached shopping as an idea, but now they have become too successful in the way the automobile became too successful. They are so powerful that they overwhelm everything else—there is nothing strong enough to balance them."[7]

Department store chains were lured to the suburbs by shopping mall developers who offered them sweetheart deals because they brought in the traffic. Those deals would eventually include many millions of dollars in subsidies to build the stores, as well as agreements that included paying little or no rent because the department stores were the primary draw; their advertising attracted customers to the centers, which generated business for their smaller specialty stores. Although this expansion to the suburbs was the necessary strategy for the post-war era, ironically, it marked the beginning of the decline of the traditional department store— thanks to the mall itself. After all, the department store was a collection under one roof of specialty departments—apparel, footwear, home furnishings, restaurants. That sounds like the definition of a shopping mall.

Merger Mania and the Decline of Regional Identity

The latter part of the 1980s was marked by retail-merger mania. In 1986, Campeau Corporation, headed by Canadian businessman Robert Campeau, paid a highly inflated price— $3.6 billion (a lot of money at the time)—for Allied Stores Corporation (which included Jordan Marsh, Stern's, and The Bon Marché) and, less than two years later, acquired Federated Department Stores (which included Bloomingdale's, Abraham & Straus, Lazarus, Burdines', and Rich's) for an even more inflated $6.6 billion. Both deals were leveraged buyouts, which were paid for mostly by high-interest junk bonds. Faced with crushing interest costs and other problems, the Campeau empire collapsed. Thousands of retail jobs were eliminated, and corporate expenses were slashed in order to pay off the massive debt.

Ever since, the major portion of the bottom-line growth of department stores has come through acquiring rival chains and consolidating and merging divisions. The industry has contracted from more than twenty national chains in the late 1970s to just seven, including the two largest moderate chains: Federated Department Stores, which includes Macy's, Bloomingdale's, Rich's, and The Bon Marché; and May Department Stores, which includes Marshall Fields, Lord & Taylor, Robinsons-May and Hecht's. (Federated's selection of merchandise is slightly higher-priced than May's.) A couple of years ago, May folded the Kaufmann's (Pittsburgh), Filene's (Boston), and Meier & Frank (Portland, Oregon) divisions into Robinsons-May, based in Los Angeles. Many observers of the department store industry believe that it is inevitable that Federated and May will one day merge, which would represent another stage in the continuing contraction of the department store sector. Because Federated and May often have anchor stores in the same malls, if they did merge, the weaker stores in the malls would be vacated, thus creating even more space for mall owners to fill.

All this activity of sales, mergers, and closings was the inevitable result of retailing being a game of scale, where stores combine their internal operations—purchasing, staff, back office, and logistics—to cope with flat or barely rising comparable store sales. Department stores are still figuring out how to use those economies of scale and their individual brands' identities to boost them ahead of their discount competitors. They are looking at ways to adapt, improve productivity, and increase gross margins, and, perhaps, to reinvent themselves.

The industry's past reliance on consolidation has contributed to many of its current woes. The mergers have transformed regional merchants, all focused on their specific customers, into a handful of nearly identical national department store chains focused on pleasing shareholders. In the quest for fatter profits, department stores cut sales staff (damaging the last vestiges of customer service, which once had been a major customer draw), allowed stores and presentations to become boring, and introduced goods designed to appeal to the masses.

They also stopped being *department* stores. Gradually, over the years, they abdicated businesses to specialty stores, rather than compete head-on with the new entries into those classifications. As they kept shredding departments, they were department stores in name only. They have become apparel (and shoe) stores, with a smattering of non-apparel businesses such as fragrances and cosmetics. Nowhere is this more dramatic than in furniture, where department stores' share has fallen to less than 5 percent from a peak of 40 percent. Today, Wal-Mart is the leading furniture retailer in the United States. As recently as the 1970s, department stores accounted for the major portion of toy sales; today, their market share is less than 5 percent; today, discount and specialty toy retailers account for 70 percent of the market.

"Hard goods was the core business of department stores," said Robert DiNicola, chairman of the Zales jewelry chain, who began his career in the 1970s as a housewares buyer for Macy's. "Once they started to give up hard goods, they lost their core customers and the built-in traffic. That was the death knell for department stores. Not from a financial standpoint, because there were a lot of economic reasons involved in those decisions—space requirements, real estate, etc.—but from the standpoints of merchandising and the relationship with the customer. The loss of the home [furnishings] businesses was the beginning of the end for the department store as we know it today."[8]

Many time-pressed customers have long ceased to be interested in navigating through departments irrelevant to their shopping mission. In greater and greater numbers, they are opting for specialty stores that carry just what they are after. Typical of this abdication of product is the home-electronics market, where department stores have seen their market share shrink from 25 percent to about 5 percent, thanks to the emergence of Best Buy, Circuit City, Target, and Wal-Mart. Consider these numbers: According to America's Research Group, in 1991, 64 percent of those polled said they shopped department stores, 42 percent visited discounters. Ten years later, 90 percent of the country's consumers visited a Wal-Mart, Kmart, or Target in 2001; and only 28 percent a department store. In 1994, people said they spent 41.5 percent of their money in department stores; by 2003, that number had dropped to 16 percent. In 1994, discount stores accounted for 41.4 percent of spending; in 2003, that number had increased to 55 percent, with a good portion of that increase occurring since 1997.[9]

As a percentage of non-automobile retail sales in the United States, according to the Commerce Department, department stores have lost market share for eight straight years through 2002, the last full year for which figures were available. Department stores' share was 20 percent in 1993 and 1994, compared with 10.9 percent in 2001.[10] Those numbers tell us that even during the 1990s, when the economy was booming, department stores continued to struggle and to lose market share.

Total retail sales of department stores, including national chains such as Sears, Roebuck and J.C. Penney fell 5 percent to $319.3 billion in 2003 from $336.1 billion in 2000, according to the U.S. Census Bureau. While Penney and Sears saw their six-year compound annual sales growth rates ebb by 1 and 0.3 percent, respectively, Wal-Mart and Target grew by 13.4 and 12.3 percent, respectively. From 1996 to 2002, the average sales per store among department store chains slumped by 0.8 percent, and sales per gross square feet fell by 0.7 percent. The average size of department stores in gross square feet shrank 0.1 percent, while that of discounters' stores increased by 3 percent. Department stores' share of the apparel business— their single most important generator of income—has dropped from 70 to 40 percent over the past twenty years, according to the market-research firm Service Industry Research Systems Inc. of Highland Heights, Kentucky.[11]

In 2002, the last full year for which metrics are available, combined sales of eleven of the top publicly traded department stores was $130.75 billion, barely half of Wal-Mart's $245 billion. That year, sales generated by conventional and national department stores declined 3.5 percent, while super-center sales increased by 21.1 percent, so-called dollar stores by 14.7 percent, warehouse clubs by 10.3 percent, and dis-counters by 4.5 percent, according to a report by retail ana-lyst Sheri Schwartzman Eberts, who based her findings on a variety of sources, including the U.S. Commerce Department and Census Bureau, J.M, Degen & Co., and company reports. Over the last decade, supercenters produced a compound annual sales growth rate of 28.5 percent, while the depart-ment store sector eked out a minuscule 0.5 percent.[12]

Shopability

In efforts to combat this decline, department stores have been rethinking everything about their operations, including the question of what kind of store will draw consumers. Many de-partment store chains, such as Sears and the Federated group, which have essentially given up the pretense of customer ser-vice, are becoming more like discounters in pricing and store layout. Department stores that have severely reduced the num-ber of full-time employees on the sales floor must rethink where they can best deploy their people so that there is a warm (hopefully knowledgeable) body to help out the customer and how those salespeople can separate that customer from her money by selling her the product that she wants.

To facilitate the movement of customers, many depart-ment store retailers are installing larger, easy-to-read signs that are reminiscent of the kind one normally sees at dis-count stores. Paco Underhill notes that today's time-pressed shoppers have "grown accustomed to stores where every-thing for sale is on open display, and they expect all the in-formation they need will be out in the open, too. Nobody wants to wait for a clerk to point them in the right direction, or explain some new product."[13]

Many stores are set up so that customers and clerks can use scanners, located in various parts of the store, to verify the prices (including the latest markdowns) on items. Federated is also testing portable scanning devices.

Federated and other chains are looking at rearranging their floor space to copy the layouts found in the discount apparel department stores of Kohl's, which combines the low-cost structure of a discounter with the brands of a department store. Kohl's, based in Menomonee Falls, Wisconsin, puts a great emphasis on speed and convenience. At an average size of eighty-five thousand square feet (half the size of a traditional department store), Kohl's stores are usually freestanding in smaller strip centers, which makes them easier to get into and out of. Kohl's is famous for its oval racetrack design, which promotes faster movement through the store, and centralized checkout stations, which save the customer time.

While making shopping faster and easier for customers, Federated and other retailers are, paradoxically, making major investments in renovations in order to make their stores the kind of destinations that they used to be—places where people are encouraged to spend hours to shop and partake of other features. There are seating areas with plasma-screen televisions, controlled by customers. The juniors' shops have beverage vending machines, video games, snacks, photo booths, and cybercafés.

Retailers setting aside space in their stores for day-care facilities is hardly a new concept. In 1927, Frederick & Nelson wanted to make shopping easier for women with children. The fourth floor of the store included a children's hairdressing salon, a lounge where mothers could care for their babies, and a kindergarten, which became a haven for both parents and children. The kindergarten included a playroom, sandbox, picture books, and toys.

Under the umbrella of "everything old is new again," department stores are back in the child-care business in an effort to get—and keep—mom in the store without having to worry about Junior. According to some industry estimates, the average shopper spends one to two hours shopping; mothers with small children spend less than one hour. Rich's-Macy's successfully tested a baby-sitting center in one of its stores in the Atlanta suburbs, and has since expanded it to other stores in the chain. Rich's found that parents usually kept their children in the child centers for the entire two hours they were allotted by the store.

Customer Loyalty: R.I.P.

Loyalty to a department store seems like such a quaint idea in these times. There was a time when consumers identified with a particular store, lured by its atmosphere, product assortment, prices, and service. In New York, there were Macy's shoppers and there were Abraham & Strauss shoppers. In Philadelphia, there were Wanamaker shoppers and Strawbridge & Clothier shoppers. But loyalty left town with the one-day-take-an-additional-50-percent-off-at-the-cash-register sale. The essence of loyalty emanates from the idea that one is paying a fair price for the item purchased. Alas, in their efforts to battle the discounters, department stores have abandoned that tacit agreement. Today's department store shoppers know that the first price is *never* the best price.

"Department stores have confused the customer with this bombardment of convoluted pricing messages," said Robert Mang, a long-time executive veteran of the department store business. "You want to know if this week's price is the best price you're going to get. Next week's price might be better or last week's price might have been better. I keep hearing about the reinvention of the department store, but I'm still looking for the model. Where is it?"[14]

Compare the situation in the United States with that of the United Kingdom, where department store anchors still flourish in many cities for a variety of reasons, including laws that stipulate that stores can discount only items that have been in the stores at full price for at least a month. Thus a sale is *really* a sale. This situation is mandated by the government, but it has at least promoted a uniform set of ground rules. Retailers are thus compelled to have to compete on criteria—such as service and selection—other than price.

In the United States, consolidations and mergers have extinguished much of the excitement that was once a part of the department store experience. Shoppers are bored with what they see, which is often a sea of sameness, a lack of variety in merchandise, because buyers, under pressure to deliver margins, are not in a position to be adventurous. The lack of distinction among stores is a result of short-term, bottom-line pressures: Numbers have to be met in the current quarter, as well as the current month and week. When you need to show profits, you tend to play it safe, depending on the tried-and-true suppliers—the ones that everyone else depends on. Result: little creativity or fashion excitement.

The core problem is an absence—with rare exceptions—of a merchandising vision.

"At department stores, there has been a push and shove between merchants and financial people; the financial people won. As a result, the department store lost touch with the consumer," said Tony Margolis, chief executive officer of Tommy Bahama, the men's and women's sportswear apparel company.[15] Margolis has been an executive in the apparel industry for several decades. His Generra Sportswear line was a major young men's fashion company in the 1980s and early 1990s, selling primary to department stores. When he and his partners started Tommy Bahama in 1992, they shunned selling to most department stores, preferring to do business only with upscale retailers such as Nordstrom, Neiman Marcus, and Saks, smaller specialty apparel stores, and their own Tommy Bahama stores.

Still, department stores are trying to reinvent their category; some are even taking the "radical" approach of adding more departments. Macy's reintroduced an upscale home electronics department. Its parent company, Federated, is testing 1,500-square foot LensCrafters optical boutiques in several of its Bon-Macy's, Bloomingdale's, and Macy's East stores. In 2003, Saks, Inc. stocked toys from the troubled FAO Schwarz chain in its Saks Fifth Avenue, Proffitt's, and Carson Pirie Scott divisions. For the holiday 2003 shopping season, Sears, which once ruled the toy world before the advent of Toys "R" Us, installed temporary KB Toys shops in six hundred of its stores, based on the success it had had the year before with KB shops in seventy-seven Sears stores. Marshall Field's placed Creative Kidstuff shops—run by the Minneapolis-based specialty toy retailer—in twenty-one of its stores in Minnesota, Michigan, and Wisconsin.

Will these new departments have any impact on a consumer who knows that she can get buy these goods cheaper at a Target, Wal-Mart, or Best Buy? Probably not. Consumers tend to buy products at retailers that demonstrate a long-term commitment to the product, which means lots of inventory, sharp pricing, and the occasional knowledgeable salesperson. Department stores can no longer offer any of those selling points.

The surviving department store chains have plenty of cash, so they will be around for a while. Most of them carry less debt than a decade ago and will be able to hold on for the foreseeable future. How that cash is used will determine their fate. Department stores have to stand for something in the mind of the consumer by defining themselves through the products they offer the marketplace. They need a long-term commitment to cultivate new customers, particularly the next generation of consumers. Some observers believe that the eighteen-to-thirty-four cohort is taking another look at the traditional department stores, which are experimenting with different lures, such as separate entrances that lead right into apparel departments so that consumers don't have to wade through other departments. But the reality is that when most consumers under the age of forty think of a general merchandise store with lots of departments under one roof, they think of Wal-Mart or Target.

Meet Me at the Altar: Sears and J.C. Penney

The retail revolution has taken its toll on one of the most venerable names in retail: Sears, Roebuck and Co. This company's history is a quintessential case study of the changing nature of retail, and how to adapt—or fail to adapt—to those changes. In 1893, a salesman named Richard Warren Sears teamed up with Alvah Curtis Roebuck, a young watchmaker, to offer the American consumer a 196-page catalog offering a vast cross-section of goods, including clothing, home furnishings, bicycles, cream separators, jewelry, and musical instruments. Within a decade, Sears overtook Montgomery Ward, which had a twenty-year head start, to become the country's top retailer.

Sears was one of the most dominant companies in America. "The network of factories selling products to Sears and the means of financing and moving goods became so large and complex that the company became a full-fledged working economy unto itself," according to author Donald R. Katz, who declared that Sears "encompassed more of the basic functions of a capitalist economy—from extraction, to fabrication, to distribution and consumption, from finance to communications—than any company before it."[16] He could just as well have been describing the Wal-Mart chain of today.

Sears's internal systems were admired across industries. According to company legend, when Henry Ford was investigating procedures for streamlined, efficient assembly-line production, he visited Sears to study a time-scheduling system for its mail-order business that had been designed in-house by an employee named Otto Doering. Ford borrowed that system when he began manufacturing the first Model T in 1903.

In the mid-1960s Sears management decided to target a more affluent middle class by emphasizing higher-quality, higher-priced merchandise, including more fashionable apparel, while de-emphasizing its lower-quality, lower-priced goods, essentially ceding that niche to the discount stores—Wal-Mart, Kmart, and Target. Since being dethroned by Wal-Mart as the nation's leading retailer in 1991, Sears has been adrift. In the 1990s, it ran an advertising campaign that played up its "softer side," including apparel and other soft goods, but all that strategy managed to accomplish was to take attention away from its core strength: hard goods such as tools and home appliances. From that time on, Sears has gone through a series of chief executive officers, strategies, images, emphases, and identities, prompting the ultimate question from the old TV game show *To Tell the Truth:* "Will the real Sears, Roebuck and Co. please stand up?" In the fall of 2001, Sears chief executive Alan Lacy told a meeting of retail stock analysts that it was no longer a department store: "We had historically been a department store and it's not working in this day and age."[17]

For many years, Sears, like other department stores, used its own internal credit cards operation as a profit center, particularly in the carrying of big purchases. Store chains that operate their own internal card divisions own the balances due on their cards, as well as fees and interest. By the same token, they are on the hook if the bill is not paid. If they outsource their credit divisions to customers such as GE Capital, they receive either a fee or a small percentage of each transaction. These cards can also help in marketing because they help record information about previous purchases that can be used to target selected products to specific cardholders/customers.

Sears's credit card business accounted for 60 percent of profits—$1.5 billion on sales of $33.75 billion in 2002—a figure that was considerably greater than other retailers'. Some 40 percent of that credit came from appliance sales. Sears was also among the top three issuers of MasterCard credit cards. In a surprise move in the summer of 2003, Sears sold its credit and financial products business to Citigroup for $32 billion, which allowed Sears to pay off almost all of its debt and cleared the books for the company to concentrate on being a retailer, rather than a bank in the guise of a retailer.

In 2002, in a move to emphasize apparel and attract a more upscale customer, Sears acquired the catalog and Internet retailer Lands' End for $1.9 billion in cash. The acquisition was both interesting and ironic. Sears, of course, was famous for its catalog, which it discontinued in 1993. Now it is back in the catalog business.

In its stores, Sears, like many retailers, is emulating the model of Kohl's, particularly in locating new stores in freestanding spaces. This concept is becoming increasingly viable for every type of retail category because it comes with several advantages: Rents are generally cheaper and operating costs can be significantly lower because the retailers don't have to pay shared utility costs for common areas. And since shoppers are more likely to go to a freestanding store for a specific item, sales per square foot are typically higher than in mallbased stores. The stand-alone stores appeal to busy people who say they don't have time to spend browsing through a mall's myriad stores. "People want to go in and out, not spend a lot of time at the mall," says Walter Loeb, an independent retail analyst in New York. "Long term, you're going to see more and more freestanding stores open."[18]

In 2003, Sears opened the first of five pilot stores in a new format called "Sears Grand" stores, which were not part of large shopping malls. Because of the national slowdown in the construction of regional malls, Sears needed to find other avenues of store expansion, so it opened in September 2003 in the Salt Lake City suburb of West Jordan, plunging right into the belly of the beast—surrounded by Wal-Mart, Sam's Club, Kohl's, Lowe's, Circuit City, and Bed Bath & Beyond. The Sears Grand stores, aimed at the time-starved shopper, carry the typical Sears selection of products and services, but also stock products that a typical Sears doesn't carry, such as CDs and DVDs, pet supplies, and books, as well as groceries.

One must give Sears's management credit for trying to figure out where Sears belongs in the retail world. But after all is said and done, the question remains: What is Sears? In apparel and other soft goods, it's not a Kohl's. In everything else, it's not Wal-Mart or Target.

And in appliances, one of its core categories, it might not be Home Depot or Lowe's either. Those two category killers, in a strategy to extend their reach and to give customers another reason to visit their stores, represent a serious challenge to Sears, where appliances, led by its Kenmore brand, have traditionally been a strength. Sears sells some $7 billion worth of refrigerators, ranges, washers and dryers, and microwaves, representing 22 percent of its 2002 sales of $31.5 billion. Much of Sears's income comes from extended appliance-repair contracts, which represent the core of its business.

According to market research firm Stevenson Co., Sears's market share in unit sales in appliances dropped almost three percentage points between 2001 and 2002, from 41.4 percent to 38.5 percent, while Lowe's and Home Depot each gained more than two points, to 13.7 percent and 6.4 percent, respectively.[19] (Best Buy also takes a bite out of the appliances business.) This erosion of market share has come about because Lowe's and Home Depot can match Sears on price, service, and selection, and many of their freestanding locations are superior to the locations of Sears's 870 stores (compared with 1,700 Home Depot stores and almost a thousand Lowe's stores), most of which are still in malls.

Adding to the challenge, market research has shown that consumers believe that Lowe's and Home Depot offer better prices and a greater selection of brands. Some consumers believe Sears sells only its Kenmore brand, although in reality it sells all the major brands. Sears has responded by reducing regular prices on some merchandise while bringing in new low-priced products, which are the specialty of the home-improvement retailers.

Another reason that the big-box stores have lured customers away from Sears is that they stock inventory; customers usually can make their purchase and take their appliance home on the same day or, at the latest, the next day, if the goods are stored in nearby warehouses. Sears has responded by increasing its in-store inventory.

J.C. PENNEY HAS ALSO gone through its own ups and downs. Company founder James Cash Penney, who was born on a small farm outside Hamilton, Missouri, was hired in 1898 to work for Guy Johnson and Thomas Callahan, who operated several Golden Rule dry-goods stores in Colorado and Wyoming. Young Penney invested $2,000 and was made a one-third partner with Johnson and Callahan. He and his wife and infant son moved to the frontier mining town of Kemmerer, Wyoming, where he opened his first store on April 14, 1902, in a one-room frame building located between a laundry and a boarding house, just off the main business district of the town. By 1904, Penney was a one-third partner in two more Golden Rule stores in Wyoming. Three years later, he bought out his partners and set out to open a chain of stores throughout the Rockies.

(The Golden Rule name was more than a marketing strategy, it embodied his philosophical and religious beliefs. Because Jim Penney, a devout Christian, was morally opposed to the idea of credit, his was a "cash-only" store—a stand he maintained until 1958, when he was overruled by the board.)

Penney would offer customers quality merchandise at the lowest possible prices, and build his business on customer service, thrift, shrewd buying practices, and a growing team of store managers and salesmen, whom he called "associates." By 1912, there were thirty-four Golden Rule Stores, with sales in excess of $2 million, headquartered in Salt Lake City, Utah. The following year, the chain changed its name to avoid confusion with other Golden Rule stores, and was incorporated as the J.C. Penney Company Inc. In 1914, the headquarters were moved to New York City to be closer to the major sources of merchandise.

In 1917, at the height of this success, Penney surprised his associates by stepping down as president. At age forty-two, he became the company's first Chairman of the Board, serving as the living symbol of the Penney philosophy. He lived to the ripe old age of ninety-six, passing away in 1971. Today, in the rotunda of the chain's home office in the Dallas suburb of Plano, Texas, a visitor is greeted by a nine-foot-tall bronze statue of the founder, dressed in a double-breasted suit and bow-tie. His left hand holds the familiar fedora hat he wore in his later years, while his right hand—oversized even for this statue—is extended to greet the visitor. A salesman even from beyond the grave.

Up until 1950, J.C. Penney was largely a decentralized company of more than 1,600 small stores in small towns all over America. As Americans began migrating to the suburbs, the Penney company moved with them. By the end of the 1950s, many of the stores were in shopping malls, which put them in direct competition with other national chains. Penney's move to the malls signaled a broadening of its merchandise offerings as the retailer began stocking sporting goods, appliances, hardware, and services such as restaurants, portrait studios, and auto maintenance. In 1993, it was the largest retail catalog company in the United States.

But by the mid-1990s, Penney had fallen on difficult times. In the fall of 2000, the retailer brought in noted turnaround artist Allen Questrom, the former chief executive officer of Federated Stores and Barneys, to revive the company that had slipped to the number five position among U.S. retailers. Continuing the contraction that had begun under his predecessors, Questrom cut more than a hundred stores, bringing the total to just over one thousand (with an additional one hundred expected to open over the next few years), and centralized the company's merchandising, buying, and pricing operation. In the pre-Questrom, decentralized J.C. Penney, store managers were given a lot of responsibility for their stores—for everything from buying to fixtures. Today, virtually every decision is determined at the Plano headquarters.

In 2004, Penney became more focused on its core business when it sold its 2,800-store Eckerd drugstore chain for $4.53 billion to two buyers, CVS and Jean Coutu Group. Like Sears, Penney sold its profitable credit card business.

It seems inevitable that the world does not need both Penney's and Sears, and there could be increased pressure for a merger—something that almost happened in the late 1990s. The idea was that Sears would sell exclusively hard goods while Penney's would sell only soft goods. But there were concerns that the Federal Trade Commission might block the plan because the two chains have stores in many of the same malls. Nevertheless, there is still no need for two sub-moderate department stores in a mall. A merger could happen in the next five years; it could happen in the next five minutes, but chances are good that it will happen at some time.

The Future of Department Stores

Further consolidation in the department store business is inevitable. For example, in the spring of 2004, May Department Stores acquired the 62-store Marshall Fields' chain from Target Corporation for $3.24 billion in cash. May's bid topped that of Federated Department Stores, the only other suitor for Marshall Fields. Federated, with close to $1 billion in cash, will almost certainly buy another chain; it's not a matter of *if*, but *when*. The inevitability of consolidation is adding to the pressures on traditional shopping malls, who will be faced with more and more vacancies as the merged department store companies close duplicate stores. Smart shopping mall developers have responded to this situation by becoming much more creative in their use of space. Department stores will continue to have a place in malls, but these traditional players will be joined by category killers, discount chains, supermarkets, and warehouse stores. For these retailers, growth must come from somewhere. Where that growth takes place will strongly influence the future of our consumer culture.

6

Growth

Expanding Their Reach

The brilliant moves we occasionally make would not
have been possible without the prior dumb ones.

—Stanley Goldstein

CATEGORY KILLERS and big-box retailers must grow; if
not, they will eventually die. Wall Street demands it.

Fortunately for these retailers, several factors—including
the shrinking influence of the traditional department store,
the consolidation among the surviving department stores,
and the uncertain future of Sears and Penney—have opened
up a treasure trove of growth opportunities. Category killers
and big discounters are experimenting with a variety of store
formats, sizes, and locations—including freestanding locations, power centers, inner city sites, and traditional so-called
full-price malls that offer ready access to densely populated
urban and suburban markets, where developable real estate
often is at a premium.

Category killers have been a key disruptive factor in the
growing weakness of traditional shopping malls, which have

been looking for ways to reinvent themselves and to find ways to grow after a fifty-plus-year run of success. There has been a dramatic drop in the number of malls that have either recently been built or are on the drawing board. According to the International Council of Shopping Centers, only eleven malls were built in 2001, eight in 2002 and 2003, and just six in 2004, and thirteen in 2004 and 2005. (During the industry's peak, forty-seven large malls opened between 1990 and 1992.) After a decade of consolidation, the ten largest mall real-estate investment trusts now control 47 percent of all malls.[1]

The weakness of department stores is threatening the future of the malls. The problem is that the department stores are still a crucial element of success in a mall because they are the biggest tenants in terms of occupying real estate, drawing traffic, and generating sales volume. A developer who wants to build a new mall must line up the right department store anchor. But some developers are questioning the old conventional wisdom of entering into long-term leasing deals with department store anchors at below-market cost, under the assumption that the anchors will bring in the crowds. Today's reality is that department stores, which continue to lose market share, are not the traffic draws they used to be.

In the old days, a lender would finance a shopping center solely on the terms that the developer had worked out with the anchor stores. "You could borrow enough to finance your whole center based on your anchor stores' deals," explains Kemper Freeman, owner of the Bellevue Square Shopping Center near Seattle, and a past president and current trustee of ICSC.[2] "The industry overdrove the major department stores." adds Freeman. "We kept adding shopping centers faster than the department stores needed space. The first sign of that was when a developer would go to a major retailer and say 'I'm doing a new mall,' and the major would say, 'That's nice; we currently don't need any new stores.' The developer would say, 'You don't understand. We need you to be there.' Developers would keep offering incentives. The standard would be to give the anchor $25 million."

As a result, "Over time, our industry grew so fast, we started to drag the department stores into markets and into stores they didn't need," says Freeman. "We grew them faster than they should have grown. We've overbuilt the whole industry. We're part of their demise." The problem, Freeman explains, is that the real estate represents only 10 percent of a department store's costs of operating in the mall. "Ninety percent of their costs still exist, even if we built the building and make it free. Those 'free' stores aren't free. The department stores aren't the best negotiators in the world. They were given unbelievable deals from the developers, who needed them to be able to make their deal. Developers would ask the management of department stores: 'What do I need to get you to want to make the deal?'"

Freeman cites an example of one mall developer that paid a retailer more than $40 million to not only build that retailer an anchor store, but also to pay for stock, staffing, and all the expenses necessary to run the store for two years. If no customers ever bought even one item during those two years, the retailer had the right to close that store without any liability. Someone once asked the CEO of that anchor store how he was able to get such one-sided deals from developers. "It isn't me," the CEO admitted with a grin. "It's the developers. I wouldn't have the balls to ask for the things they give me of their own volition."[3]

Developers no longer want to make those kinds of deals. They are also faced with the turnover of specialty stores—be they chain stores or local mom-and-pop operations. At the Simon Property Group, which owns and operates almost two hundred malls throughout North America, seven of its top ten tenants a decade ago have changed. It is never a matter of *if* a retailer vacates a mall, it's a matter of *when*.

Anchors Away

With the weakening of department stores, shopping mall developers are asking themselves some basic questions, including this one: "What will constitute a major anchor in the future?" Will it be a theme restaurant, movie theater, bowling alley, government building, supermarket, discounter, or big-box category killer? They will have plenty of opportunity to find out because, over the next ten years, upward of eight hundred anchor spots in malls will become vacant; half of them could be occupied by discounters.

For expansion-minded discounters, these shopping mall sites come with both benefits and drawbacks. On the plus side, the properties are well-established, and already come with the requisite parking, lighting, and other infrastructure needs. In addition, the set-up offers greater in-store traffic and high sales per square foot. On the down side, many abandoned department stores generally comprise more than one floor, which forces discounters to adapt from their traditional single-floor layout. In addition, traditional shopping malls involve higher costs for logistics, because loading and unloading merchandise is not as efficient (or as convenient) as it is in freestanding stores.

Power Centers

So-called "power center" malls are a "murderers' row" of category killers of various sizes, including Wal-Mart and Target. As populations shift, new homes are built and new communities are created, old mall locations are abandoned and new locations spring up to accommodate the changes in demographics. One of the advantages of power centers is that shoppers can park close to their store of destination, and get in and out quickly.

Arguably the first power center was the 330,000-square-foot 280 Metro Center in Colma, California, located across Highway 280 from the Serramonte shopping center in Daly City. It was developed in the 1970s, when the original first-generation regional shopping centers started to show their age and discounting was in full bloom. Actually, the mall was not originally dubbed a "power center"; it was called a "promotional center," said Merritt Sher, the mall's original developer. Sher created an attractive tenant mix with a variety of leading discount specialty retailers including Big 5 sporting goods, Pacific Stereo, and Wallpapers to Go. "It was a component business. Instead of having a dominant supermarket anchor or a dominant department store anchor, we had a half a dozen anchors of varying sizes and shapes, to create a critical mass to be the largest selection of that type of retail within a regional market."

After several years running 280 Metro Center as a promotional center, Sher and his team decided to change the marketing of the center by renaming it a *power center*, a term that made it easier to sell to retailers and to consumers. "We wanted to tell the world that the time has come for these kinds of stores to be aggregated in one place," said Sher. "Twenty-five years ago, I told the International Council of Shopping Centers that someday there will be freeway off-ramps for those kinds of [category killer] stores. That was considered heresy. In those days, developers were only building those kinds of stores across from malls, which were the draw. On the other hand, we built near a freeway off-ramp and bunched all these stores together."[4]

Today, 280 Metro Center is owned by Kimco Realty Corporation, based in Hyde Park, New York, which owns 560 shopping centers in the United States and Canada, including Parkway Power Center in the Southcenter area near Seattle. The current tenant mix at 280 Metro includes Home Depot,

Kids "R" Us, Marshall's, Nordstrom Rack, Barnes & Noble, and Bed Bath & Beyond.

Smaller Store Formats

In their constant quest to find places to add stores, most category killers are taking a two-pronged approach. They are either building larger stores in areas with an abundance of available undeveloped property, or building smaller stores in small-town downtowns or in densely populated urban communities.

Shoppers are spending less time at the mall—an average of 2.9 hours a month in 2003, compared with four hours in 2000, according to consultant Stillerman Jones & Co.[5] Because many shoppers are reacting negatively to dealing with big superstores full of jammed aisles and backed-up checkout lines, they are turning to smaller specialty stores, where they can get in, buy what they're looking for, and get out. In response, category killers are opening small, easier-to-shop, neighborhood stores to attract these time-pressed consumers. Although smaller stores translate to lower costs, the challenge for category killers is to find ways to extract the highest possible number of sales in a limited space.

Home Depot, which has about two-thirds of its stores concentrated in the nation's fifty largest markets, has been opening stores in rural and secondary markets such as Iron Mountain, Michigan, (population 8,644), and Barboursville, West Virginia (population 2,742). Those moves are based on company research of areas that are underserved by neighboring Home Depot stores or competitors, but that have a population with above-average household income and a high percentage of home ownership. In the mid-1990s, most Home Depot stores occupied 160,000 square feet; today, they are each about 115,000 square feet.

Home Depot is also opening smaller urban stores, dubbed "Depot Lite," in inner cities. (In fact, most of Home Depot's newer stores are being built in urban markets.) The first of these units—a two-story, glass-fronted emporium with escalators—opened in 2001 in the upscale Lincoln Park neighborhood of Chicago. In 2004, Home Depot opened two pedestrian-friendly stores in Manhattan, including one on Third Avenue at 59th Street, near Bloomingdale's, and another on 23rd Street between Fifth Avenue and the Avenue of the Americas. In its quest for additional viable retail sites, Home Depot, in spring 2004, announced it was acquiring as many as nineteen Kmart stores (many of them in urban areas) from Kmart Holding Corp., with the intention of converting them into Home Depot stores. The company has also been experimenting with new formats, such as its Landscape Supply stores and its upscale Expo home-design stores, which offer do-it-yourselfers sharper prices on items such as granite countertops and window treatments.

Lowe's, which has just under a thousand stores—compared with Home Depot's 1,700—is expanding aggressively into metropolitan areas long dominated by Home Depot. Some industry observers maintain that if Home Depot and Lowe's keep up this same rate of growth, they soon will saturate the category's capacity for big-box stores. Whether that happens in 2004 or 2010, the two chains will eventually be forced to cannibalize their existing operations—including closing old stores and replacing them with new state-of-the-art venues, which will be influenced by changing market conditions, consumer tastes, lifestyle changes, and other factors. Wal-Mart has been doing that for years by replacing its traditional stores with larger SuperCenters, which combine a massive supermarket component with the usual general merchandise.

In 2002, Best Buy began opening smaller thirty-thousand-square-foot stores in smaller markets (under two hundred thousand residents) such as Wichita Falls, Texas, and Kokomo, Indiana. By way of comparison, the typical Best Buy in urban areas is forty-five thousand square feet. These smaller units are expected to account for about half of the chain's new stores, until Best Buy hits its projected saturation point of about 650 large and mid-size outlets in 2005. The stores have the same warehouse feel as Best Buy's larger outlets, but the aisles are narrower, and there is little room for office furniture or small appliances. Unlike Circuit City, which stopped selling appliances in 2000, Best Buy still offers an extensive line of refrigerators and stoves, as well as computer software, big-screen TVs, camcorders, and digital video disc players.

Circuit City, too, has changed its approach. It has spent more than $100 million in redesigning some stores, relocating others, and expanding into new locations. The stores were converted to self-service operations, and designed to make it easier for customers to take the merchandise off the shelves.

Staples Superstores, generally located in suburban malls, typically carry more than 7,500 office supply items in twenty thousand square feet of space, while Staples.com offers forty-five thousand products and a wide variety of business services. Beginning in 2002, Staples began launching stores that were 17 percent smaller—twenty thousand square feet, down from the original twenty-four thousand—and did not have the old warehouse feel. The traditional high red racks were replaced with low gray shelves, which offered more accessible sight lines, showing the full scope of merchandise. Customers had complained that they had been unable to locate the items that they were looking for, and had difficulty finding help to wait on them. In the smaller stores, with everything in plain view, customers need less help from the staff.

Staples used to have a floor plan that featured aisles plotted out like city streets in a linear-grid pattern. They have since changed the floor plan to the oval racetrack design—initially popularized by Kohl's—that promotes faster movement and time-savings while inviting shoppers to stroll past merchandise displays and pick up impulse items. Staples also made better use of its space by discontinuing slow-moving, unprofitable consumer items such as Britney Spears back-packs, pens shaped like vegetables, printers for under $100, child-oriented computer games, and educational software.

Even Starbucks is looking to go smaller. The coffee retailer has been adding hundreds of drive-through windows in stores in North America, and is testing a drive-through-only format in several markets. Since 1998, Starbucks has been expanding into inner-city locations in partnership with basketball legend Earvin "Magic" Johnson's Johnson Development Corporation, which also operates theaters, T.G.I. Friday's restaurants, and other retail businesses in urban areas.

Costco has been experimenting with a home furnishings and décor warehouse, called Costco Home, which it opened at the end of 2002 in the Seattle suburb of Kirkland. Selling exclusively to Costco Wholesale members, the store—the company's first warehouse to carry a single merchandise category—offers about three thousand items, including top-grain leather sofas, furniture, bedding, desks, limited-edition artwork, tapestries, carpeting, window fashions, and other products and services for the home. In 2003, Costco toyed with the idea of opening a gourmet shop, to be called Costco Fresh, which was to feature gourmet groceries and include a pharmacy, bakery, olive bar, deli, café, garden center, and photo and optical departments. Products would be packaged in smaller quantities, and membership would be required. Although the company opted to put off the project, Costco continues experimenting with fresh-food offerings at its warehouse stores.

Wal-Mart is also adding smaller stores. Since 1998, the company has been operating its Neighborhood Market stores, which average about forty-five thousand square feet—larger than many supermarkets, but smaller than the average Wal-Mart—in rural areas deemed too small for SuperCenters. Dubbed "Small-Marts" by retail analysts, the fifty-plus Neighborhood Markets are sprinkled throughout the south and southwest, primarily in Oklahoma, Arkansas, Texas, Mississippi, Tennessee, Florida, and Alabama. Neighborhood markets carry about twenty-four thousand products, compared with a hundred thousand in the SuperCenters. The stores stock the usual supermarket inventory of groceries, over-the-counter drugs, and beauty products, as well as prepared foods, pastries, drive-through pharmacies, and half-hour film processing (thanks to research that discovered that half of all women shoppers are carrying an undeveloped roll of film in their purses). Stores also have self-check-out lanes. Wal-Mart has tried to create an old-fashioned general store touch with its honor-system coffee bar. The jury is still out as to whether the Neighborhood Markets will work for Wal-Mart. Because it is selling food (accounting for 65 percent of sales) just like the competition, the Neighborhood Market doesn't appear to be offering any inherent advantage to shoppers.

Dollar Stores

Wal-Mart has also been experimenting with one of the hottest concepts in retail: the dollar store. Small variety stores, conveniently located in neighborhoods all across the country, dollar stores—the anti-big-box—represent the virtual rebirth of the five-and-ten store that Frank Winfield Woolworth created back in 1879. The dollar store concept, as its name suggests, is built around price, and is redefining the category killer model. Customers perceive these stores to have lower prices—comparable to Wal-Mart prices—and to be more convenient because they're smaller. Although they were originally intended to attract families with income under $35,000, dollar stores are now drawing more affluent customers. According to an A.C. Nielsen survey of people who shopped dollar stores at least once a year from 2000 to 2003, the demographic with the highest rate of growth was households with annual income of at least $70,000.[6]

These efficient stores, which feature a tightly-edited assortment of merchandise, attract a customer who doesn't have the time or energy to shop a large retail space or even to hike across the football-field-size parking lot. Although many of these stores started out small—3,500 to 6,000 square feet or so—some of the big chains are now building "superstores," ranging from 9,000 to 12,000 square feet.

Dollar stores generate tens of billions of dollars in sales through more than twenty thousand locations throughout the country. In recent years, these stores have achieved annual double-digit increases in volume and net income, according to industry estimates. Some sixty million households in the United States will shop at dollar stores this year, and 28 percent of American consumers surveyed said that they shop at these variety stores at least once a month, according to A.C. Nielsen. Total industry sales are projected to hit $26 billion in 2007.[7] The stores—many of which do not accept credit cards—have become more and more popular every year. They are simple, no-frills retail spaces selling housewares, candy and food, toys, party goods, cleaning supplies, health and beauty aids, and other items at low prices.

The stores are targeting the same middle-income women who shop at Wal-Mart, Target, and Kmart. In fact, many of the dollar stores are located in low-rent neighborhoods or rural areas near those big-box discounters, and draw the traffic to strip centers, where many of them are located. These retailers draw customers from a very small radius—one to three miles—so, as they expand, they are not afraid of cannibalizing their existing stores. We are also seeing them attract middle- and upper-income shoppers who are interested in saving a dollar or two.

The biggest players in this category include: Dollar General, with annual sales of more than $6.7 billion and 6,700 stores nationally; Family Dollar, based in Charlotte, North Carolina, with sales of $4.1 billion and more than 5,100 locations. Dollar Tree Stores, based in Chesapeake, Virginia, which operates about 2,500 stores, with sales of $3 billion, and also runs stores under the names Dollar Express, Dollar Bills, Only One Dollar, and Only $One.[8]

Wal-Mart has responded by installing an experimental section in its SuperCenters—called "Pennies-n-Cents"—stocked with goods that cost a dollar or less. Target is doing a similar test in a department it calls "The One Spot," which stocks a variety of items from food to batteries. Exxon Mobil is trying out the concept in its gas-station-based convenience stores, as are the Kroger supermarket chain and the Walgreens drugstore chain.

Inner-City Retailing

The move of category killers to smaller, more compact inner-city locations is bringing about a Renaissance in retailing in urban neighborhoods that have been underserved for years, sometimes decades.

Historically, big-box retailers had shied away from locating in urban neighborhoods because of the high real estate and construction costs, the hassle of complicated and lengthy permit processes, and higher-than-average crime rates. But today, in many urban municipalities, we are seeing the flourishing of private-public partnerships to help retailers navigate the minefield of government regulation, and to help them secure tax incentives and other benefits. There are tens of billions of dollars in sales opportunities in inner cities, largely being missed by retailers. Even if the actual number is half that amount, that is still a lot of business left on the table.

In 2003, the South Central section of Los Angeles saw the first meaningful development of a commercial area since the riots it endured in 1992. Developers built this project with $7 million in federal and municipal grants and loans. Dubbed Chesterfield Square, the shopping core is located about a mile from the corner of Florence and Normandie Avenues, where trucker Reginald Denny was beaten during the riots. The

250,000-square-foot retail development, which is anchored by a 132,000-square-foot Home Depot, also includes Starbucks, Food 4 Less, Subway, Radio Shack, McDonald's, International House Of Pancakes, Vision Beauty, and VIP Music. The developer said he was convinced the project could work when he read a 1999 study of the neighborhood by Pepperdine University, which revealed that the half-million people who lived within a three-mile radius of South Central were spending $900 million a year outside their neighborhood, which had an average annual household income of $37,000.[9] Within a five-mile radius, the population was about 1.2 million.

Wal-Mart has begun in earnest to expand to the inner city, despite having to deal with higher costs for construction, traffic issues, parking, and potential union concerns, all of which have an impact on the thin margins that generate its profitability. Urban Wal-Marts have to be multi-floored because one-floor Wal-Mart-sized sites are rarely available for commercial development. In January 2003, the company took over a department store space that Macy's West had abandoned in 1998 and opened a three-floor, 150,000-square-foot store at the 850,000-square-foot Baldwin Hills Crenshaw Plaza in central Los Angeles. Wal-Mart has run television and print ads that prominently feature the positive impact of this project on a community that was starving for affordable retail.

In order for the multi-level store to work, Wal-Mart had to install a special escalator/conveyor system that accommodates the oversized shopping carts that enable its customers to purchase many items at one time. Looking very much like side-by-side escalators, the escalator and cart-conveyor combination moves shoppers and their carts between floors along parallel tracks. The cart-conveyor system, long popular in Europe, where retailers have long been dealing with space limitations, is now used on a regular basis by Wal-Mart, Target, and other big box retailers. The escalator can move up to eight hundred carts an hour from floor to floor and is set up to electronically prevent carts from being taken away from the site. Many observers believe the system will help revive retail in similar urban centers because the technology allows the big boxes to be built to the right size to generate profits. At the Baldwin Hills Wal-Mart, the heaviest merchandise is displayed closest to the escalators, for the convenience of the customers.

These kinds of accommodations have become de rigueur for big-box retailers, which were loath to deviate from their standard store formats. Even as recently as the late 1990s, they were apt to make non-negotiable demands: single-level store (possibly out of scale with the neighborhood), massive parking lots, etc. These days, because of zoning regulations, pressure from neighborhood groups, and competition for sites among other retailers, big-box stores have been willing to make compromises. (In chapter 8, we will examine the response of urban and suburban communities to the expansion of big-box stores in more detail.) Their challenge is to shrink stores without shrinking sales by "editing" the store's merchandise mix and customizing it to local tastes.

What is happening in South Central Los Angeles is being played out in many other parts of the country, where urban areas are being revitalized by category killers and other big-box retailers looking for new places to expand. In Stamford, Connecticut, in 2003, Target broke ground on a 164,0000-square-foot store on Broad Street, joining Burlington Coat Factory, Wal-Mart, and Sam's Club, which were helping to fill a 4.2-acre, fifteen-block parcel of land at the corner of Grey-rock Place and Tresser Boulevard; the site had stood vacant for two decades, and had been called by locals, "the hole in the ground." When completed, the retail space will be complemented by the construction of 550 apartment units at Stamford Place. Wal-Mart is building a 150,000-square-foot Sam's Club warehouse store in the basement of the building, while the seventh floor will be occupied by a 150,000-square-foot Wal-Mart SuperCenter.

Not surprisingly, bookstores are sought after by developers because they attract a better-educated, more affluent customer; and the in-store cafes, meeting rooms, and author readings and other events are the ingredients for a physical center for a neighborhood's literary, social, and political interests. Borders Books is helping to revitalize parts of urban neighborhoods in Detroit and Chicago that have been underserved by major retailers. In November 2003, Borders opened an eight-thou-sand-square-foot store in the center of downtown Detroit at the Compuware Corporation's new 1.1-million-square-foot world headquarters building, the first meaningful retail devel-opment since the construction of the riverfront Renaissance Center in the 1970s. Borders is the anchor for about sixty thou-sand square feet of retail space at the corner of Woodward Avenue and Monroe Street, once the center of the city's retail core; in another era the location was anchored by the flagship of the J. L. Hudson Company department store, which, before it was closed in the 1980s and then demolished in the 1990s, filled a square block just north of where the Compuware Build-ing stands now. In Chicago, Borders is the primary retail an-chor for a mixed-use retail and residential project on the North Side. The complex, called Uptown Square, is intended to gen-trify a run-down part of town. Borders occupies twenty-five thousand square feet of the total forty thousand square feet of retail space.

AGAIN, BIG RETAILERS are faced with a growth impera-tive. In order to achieve that growth, retailers and developers are becoming as creative as they can. Even as they search for expansion in domestic locations, they also know that they must take advantage of opportunities outside the United States. International growth is a much bigger challenge, but it cannot be avoided.

7

Expansion

Paper Clips in Portugal

They change their clime, but not their mind,
who rush across the sea.

—Horace

FOR MANY YEARS, U.S.-based category killers have been seeking growth opportunities in international markets, but they have met with decidedly mixed results. They have been faced with many challenges, including the high cost of land, restrictive rules on discounting, and legally mandated limits on the number of hours in a day that a store can be open. In many developed countries, big-box stores—which, by definition, require a lot of real estate—encounter strict zoning and land-use limitations, making it more difficult to execute their strategy. In France, for example, the government has tightly regulated the number of large stores that can be opened in a particular region, because of an overriding interest in protecting existing retail businesses, particular those located in downtowns.

At the same time, it's a shrinking retail world. There are no secrets, no surprises. Consequently, we are seeing the homogenization of global retailing as retailers investigate and closely study the operations of other retailers, and then imitate them. For example, when Tesco, the U.K. supermarket chain, began competing with Carrefour in Thailand and Eastern Europe, it closely observed its France-based competitor, improved its own operations in those countries and then used what it learned to improve the Tesco stores in the United Kingdom.

Outside of North America, Carrefour is the world retail leader, particularly in France (where it controls 30 percent of the retail market) as well as in Spain, Portugal, Greece, and Italy (there are no Wal-Mart operations—yet—in any of those countries); and it is a major power in Latin America (particularly Brazil) and Asia (particularly China). Carrefour, which means "crossroad" in French, made one stab at the U.S. market in 1993, with a store in Philadelphia, but it failed to catch on. The organization, which began as a family business in 1959, has more than eleven thousand stores—including hypermarkets, supermarkets, and discount operations—in thirty countries. Roughly half of its sales come from France, with another 38 percent from the rest of Europe. Like every other retailer in the world, Carrefour is dwarfed by Wal-Mart, whose sales of $256.3 billion are about 2.5 times as large as Carrefour's 2003 sales of $79 billion.

Category killers have been in business for several years in China, Hong Kong, Philippines, Malaysia, Singapore, and Thailand, but in most of those countries, category killers are much smaller than their U.S. counterparts—sometimes as small as five thousand to seven thousand square feet. A typical example is the Shoemart chain in the Philippines, which, in addition to shoes, carries apparel, CDs, and other general merchandise. In India, a store called Nallis is considered a category killer in silk saris, and indeed, it has a decades-old reputation for the finest handwoven saris throughout India and East Asia; it has now spread its operations to the United States and Canada.

Lost In Translation

"Many of the U.S. category killers have not been particularly curious about other countries," said Joseph H. Ellis, a noted retail analyst with Goldman Sachs. "Most American retailers have myopia. We have a tendency to think that all the good ideas and concepts started here. They are slow to investigate what is abroad."[1]

It is not easy to give a blanket evaluation of how U.S. category killers are doing abroad. One must review country by country, category by category to see what's working, what isn't, and why. First of all, several countries already had their category killers in place before the U.S. retailers arrived. How effective have those indigenous category killers been? How entrenched are they in terms of market share and number of stores? How much preemptive expansion has already occurred?

"You have to look at the nature of each individual category and ask what is needed to merchandise that category," said Ellis. "For example, in electronics, are the plugs the same? In the do-it-yourself category, are door-handle specifications different? Some of the so-called issues of global sourcing don't work very well when the products are completely different in terms of the brands sold market-by-market. In Germany, GE is not going to be a hot seller. It might be Rowenta or Philips. So, U.S. category killers have to investigate who dominates those markets and what will be their access to those markets."

Some categories translate more easily than others. Food is relatively simple because the retailers are primarily buying from local sources for local needs. Starbucks doesn't deal with complex logistical issues. Assuming that the customer will like its coffee in the form that it is served, Starbucks can sell it pretty much everywhere, and it intends to do just that.

Toys "R" Us has been one of the more successful U.S. category killers in terms of exporting its retail concept abroad. For the most part, toys are universal (with the exception of some local customs and cultural issues (e.g., German shoppers buy a lot of wooden toys). Barbie doesn't have be plugged in, so retailers don't have to worry about issues of product specification. Toys "R" Us has done extremely well in England, where its sales productivity and profitability outperform any of their other regions. The retailer has been helped by the fact that the United Kingdom is understored; therefore, Toys "R" Us faced negligible competition from discounters or mass retailers of toys. In France, Germany, and Spain, there are also no dominant toy specialty stores. Toys "R" Us has done reasonably well, even in competition with established hypermarket retailers such as Carrefour, Auchan, and Géant (a division of Kazeno). In Japan, where goods are sold through several layers of middlemen, Toys "R" Us overcame initial resistance and introduced the concept of one-stop shopping.

WAL-MART WORLD-MART

Wal-Mart's international experience has been a mixed bag. Nevertheless, the international market is where the company envisions a good portion of its growth. At Wal-Mart's June 2003 shareholders meeting, John Menzer, the head of the international division said: "Today, the U.S. represents 37 percent of the gross national product of the world. That leaves 63 percent to focus on our international growth opportunities."[2]

In fiscal 2003, Wal-Mart's international sales increased by 18.6 percent to $47.5 billion, with an operating profit of $2.3 billion, an increase of 18.6 percent compared with the previous fiscal year (following an increase of 55.8 percent over the previous year). International is the second largest division, behind Wal-Mart Stores, in sales and earnings. If Wal-Mart International were a separate company, it would rank in the top 30 among *Fortune* 500 companies, based on sales. As of May 2004, the international division had more than 1,500 stores.

Wal-Mart's first foray outside the United States was in Mexico, which it entered in 1991 with a Sam's Club outside Mexico City.

Today, Wal-Mart is the biggest retailer in Mexico, with 650 units in that country, representing more than 42 percent of Wal-Mart's foreign stores. Wal-Mart accounts for 50 percent of all supermarket sales, and its dynamic discounting is credited by Mexican officials for helping to put a lid on the country's once ingrained inflation problems. Wal-Mart's operations in Mexico include regular Wal-Mart stores, Sam's Club and Bodega warehouse stores, VIPS diners (serving an extensive menu from chicken enchiladas to cheeseburgers), the Superama supermarket chain, and the Suburbia clothing and home goods store. Wal-Mart is the country's single biggest private employer, with more than one hundred thousand employees.

To illustrate Wal-Mart's impact in Mexico, one need only drive through Monterrey, where along the highway from the airport, a giant billboard features a smiling family under the words: "Now houses in front of Wal-Mart!"

After expanding into Puerto Rico in 1992, Wal-Mart began a pattern of international expansion that centered around acquiring established successful local chains. The company did that when it moved into Canada in March 1994 with the purchase of 122 failing Woolco stores. At the time, some Canadians did not appreciate another American institution steamrolling its way across the border. Wal-Mart did have problems organizing employees and meeting the national requirements for bilingual packaging, but eventually, those issues were straightened out. Wal-Mart also heeded feedback from employees in its Canadian stores, and was open to modifications if they satisfied the customers—and still made the target numbers. Whenever possible, Wal-Mart purchased products made by Canadians for Canadians.

After the initial uncertainty about Wal-Mart, Canadians have warmed up to the company. A couple of years ago, some eight hundred people in the Manitoba farming village of Onoway, near Edmonton, signed and sent in a petition to Wal-Mart asking for a store. The same thing happened in Miramichi, New Brunswick, where in the space of six weeks 11,276 people signed a petition. Both cities were hoping to bring in a Wal-Mart as a boost to their moribund local economies.

Today, Wal-Mart is the leading discount retailer in Canada, with 236 stores or 15.7 of all Wal-Mart units.

Toys "R" Us, Wal-Mart Stores Inc., and Carrefour, which have collectively opened 2,300 stores outside their home markets, are facilitating the internationalization of toys through broad, vendor-driven promotional campaigns. For example, in 2004, the Walt Disney company introduced an international blitzkrieg of stationery, backpacks, toys, and apparel based on the animated teenage super-heroine of the "Kim Possible," show on the Disney Channel. As part of an exclusive merchandising deal with Wal-Mart, Disney's "Kim Possible" line will hit the superstore chain's 2,800 U.S. stores this fall, and its 1,300 international stores in 2004.

For category killers to expand abroad, they must first research the individual markets to make sure the opportunities are there. Then they must decide how long they are willing to stick with the challenges and uncertainties of international expansion. They must also closely examine the existing competition. As the world—particularly the retail world—has gotten smaller, the best practices of dominant retailers no longer remain secret for very long. For years, international retailers have studied the best practices of U.S. retailers and, in some cases, have created carbon copies. In other cases, they have learned from the best practices of other countries in Europe or Asia, and have imported them back to their own country. There are no locally protected markets. Even before a U.S.-based category killer enters an international market, most of that retailer's best practices have influenced—or been adopted by—the local competition in that particular category. Foreign-based category killers have learned their lessons well. As a result, they have already closed those markets to significant expansion by expertly imitating what they saw in the U.S., and they have the additional advantage of being the home operator in those countries.

Do-It-Yourself

U.S.-based companies can't just arrive in a country and take market share. For example, Home Depot has not expanded to

Germany—a large, affluent market with many do-it-yourself customers—because it ran head-on into the German retailer Hornbach, which in 1968, became the first European company to open a combined construction and garden market. Hornbach studied Home Depot very closely in the 1980s, learned from the Atlanta-based home improvements retailer, and established a chain of large warehouse stores that do what Home Depot does almost as well as Home Depot does it, even down to the orange logo. Today, Hornbach has more than a hundred stores in Germany (primarily), as well as in Austria, Luxembourg, the Netherlands, the Czech Republic, and Switzerland.

"By the time Home Depot arrived in Europe, particularly Germany, they were faced with Hornbach, Obi, Praktiker, and several others," says Ellis. "Why aren't they in France? France already has a Leroy Merlin, which is a part of the Auchan Group and Castorama [France's leading do-it-yourself retailer], which is part of Kingfisher."

In the United Kingdom, the leader is the country's first national do-it-yourself chain B&Q, which was founded in March 1969 by Richard Block and David Quayle in Southampton. In 1995, after years of steady growth and acquisitions, B&Q introduced its first larger-format warehouse store and the following year opened its first store outside the United Kingdom, in Taiwan. In 1998, the chain merged with Castorama to become the largest do-it-yourself retailer in Europe. Today, there are 466 B&Q and Castorama stores in seven countries, with annual sales of $6.4 billion. And, like Home Depot, they have an orange logo.

B&Q's operations are tailor-made for its European clientele. Specifically, because few people in Europe have huge homes and decks, most of B&Q's home décor business is geared toward people who dwell in small homes and apartments.

Robert Nardelli, CEO of Home Depot, which has between 10 and 12 percent share of the $500 billion global home-improvement market, has said publicly that the chain eventually will expand to Asia and Europe, but has not indicated where or when. He has speculated that Asian expansion would probably be in the form of constructing new stores in "greenfields"—large undeveloped tracts of land. An obvious target market in Asia would be China, where the company operates two offices for sourcing proprietary products, and in 2004 opened a store-development office. China has loosened constraints on foreign retailers, who are no longer obligated to participate in join ventures with Chinese partners or secure approval from the central government for each new store. Home Depot projects the home-improvement market in China to reach $50 billion, with a compound growth rate of 20 percent.[3] Growth in Europe would most likely come from acquisitions of small existing retailers that dot a very fragmented market.

Close to home, in Canada, Home Depot has fared much better. Like other American category killers operating internationally, Home Depot has learned that, to be successful, it is imperative to appreciate the nuances not only of the country itself, but also sections of that country. For example, the Quebec stores load up on paint, wallpaper, and blinds in summer, when Quebecers tend to move; the large numbers of rental units in the province means that people there move more often.

In 2004, Home Depot doubled its presence in central and northern Mexico by acquiring the 20 stores of Home Mart Mexico, giving Home Depot a total of 39 stores in that country. The crown jewels of the Home Mart Mexico stores were the 10 in metropolitan Mexico City.

Consumer Electronics

A similar nod to local concerns was exhibited by Best Buy in 2001 when it acquired the Canadian-based Future Shop. Rather than change the store name, Best Buy kept it as Future Shop, because of its inherent brand equity. The Future Shop and Best Buy stores carry different products at different price points. Some analysts credit that move with temporarily discouraging Circuit City from expanding into Canada. That situation changed in March of 2004, when Circuit City acquired Intertan Inc., which operates almost a thousand stores and outlets in Canada under the RadioShack, Rogers Plus, and BatteryPlus names. Intertan also sells its private-label goods in the Unites States through Circuit City Superstores.

Office Products

Office products represent a category that was relatively easier to enter in overseas markets because, in much of the world, the office-supply business is broken down into two sectors:

1. **Local office supply retailers:** The middlemen between the manufacturers and the local businesses, these retailers take a large mark-up on huge assortments of merchandise in order to play local distributor for these supplies.

2. **Cash-and-carry warehouses:** The most popular concept in much of the world, the cash-and-carry warehouse predates the Costcos and Sam's Clubs by a decade or two. Two of the biggest are Metro, based in Germany, and Macro, based in the Netherlands, which are complementary to each other because they generally operate in different countries in Europe. While Costco carries four thousand SKUs, these chains generally carry eighteen thousand to twenty-thousand SKUs in a variety of categories. Because they stock a much larger assortment in large warehouses, their goods require more handling, which means they require an initial mark-up of 18 to 20 percent, as opposed to Costco's 8 to 10 percent.

Because of this arrangement, U.S.-based office-supply retailers were presented with major opportunities for growth in European markets. From the time it first entered Europe in 1992, Staples has made a number of important strategic alliances and acquisitions. In 2001, the company entered into a formal alliance with the Lyreco Group, a $1.2 billion France-based supplier, to expand its European contract business service, through which it provides customized services, including pricing, tracking and billing. In 2002, Staples acquired Guilbert, the mail-order business of the French retailer Pinault-Printemps-Redoute, for $808.7 million, which gave it a foothold in France, Italy, Spain, and Belgium, and increased its delivery sales in Europe from $50 million to $450 million overnight. (In 2002, PPR sold the Guilbert retail stores to Office Depot.) In early 2004, Staples purchased the United Kingdom–based office-products company Globus Office World Plc. from the Swiss-based Globus-Gruppe for 32.5 million pounds. Based outside of London, Globus Office World Plc. operates fifty-nine stores. Combined with its operations in Germany, Portugal, the Netherlands, and the United Kingdom, Staples runs almost two hundred stores in Europe, as well as its German Web site, Staples.de. Staples has ambitious expansion plans for Europe over the next few years.

Office Depot has been the pacesetter in this sector in Europe. Although it entered the market later than Staples, it came in with a superior strategy. In 1998, Office Depot merged with Viking Office Products, a catalog operation based in Torrance, California, which had had a presence in Europe since 1990. Viking, which was founded in 1960, made its mark by selling office products to small- and medium-sized businesses in the United States through direct marketing catalogs. Because the Viking name was well established internationally, Office Depot has continued to use that name in Austria, Belgium, France, Germany, Ireland, Italy, Japan, Luxembourg, the Netherlands, Portugal, Spain, Switzerland,

and the United Kingdom. In Central America, Office Depot is expanding through a joint venture with Mexican retailer Grupo Gigante. Stores have been added in Guatemala and Costa Rica, to go along with the more than sixty units in twenty-one cities across Mexico, as well as distribution facilities in Monterrey and Mexico City.

Japan has presented greater challenges for American office supply category killers. Like a wide variety of U.S. retailers, these category killers assumed that Japan—which in the 1990s was in the throes of a recession—would be open to their type of retailing. The country was facing declining prices of real estate and the progressive abating of protectionist laws that were intended to shield from competition the twenty thousand mom-and-pop stores that dominated a $13 billion stationery market—in which every consumer was forced to pay full price. Office Depot and OfficeMax each entered into joint venture agreements with local partners and tried to duplicate their U.S. formula in Japan. The big-box stores sold heavily discounted merchandise, a strategy that failed because the stores were too large (more than twenty thousand square feet), too American (wide aisles and signs in English), and did not cater to the Japanese consumer. For example, they stocked three-ring looseleaf binders in a country where two-ring binders were the norm. Consequently, the U.S. category killers had to purchase most of their products from the same local suppliers that were doing business with the local mom-and-pop stores. (Faced with a similar challenge of providing unconventional product specifications, J.C. Penney ultimately closed five home-furnishing stores, in part because so many products, from curtains to bedsheets, had to be made differently for Japan.)

Challenged with selling the same products as their competitors, the U.S. firms tried to get an edge on price. But some local suppliers, afraid of alienating their long-time customers, did not always give the U.S. companies their very best prices. Add to this mix Japan's astronomical rents, and it was extremely difficult for the U.S. companies to turn a decent profit.

Just as U.S. do-it-yourself stores have been outmaneuvered by European companies, U.S. office-products firms were outmaneuvered by a local Japanese firm. In 1993, Plus Corp., the country's second largest stationery maker, created a discount catalog division called Askul Corporation. The company's market research revealed there was no Japanese company catering to the needs of small businesses (thirty or fewer employees), which represented 95 percent of Japan's 6.6 million companies. "Askul," is a romanized contraction of *ashita kuru* (literally, "arrive tomorrow"), or "next-day delivery," in business idiom. The company, which spun off from Plus in 1997, has proven to be a worthy adversary. Today, the U.S. office-products companies have learned from their experience in Japan, and are operating stores in the five-thousand-square-foot range, about 20 percent the size of their U.S. units.

Staples, in particular, has fared well in Canada, where it merged with Business Depot Ltd. to form Staples: The Business Depot Ltd., the country's largest office products superstore chain. Operating stores in every province under the Staples Business Depot and Bureau En Gros names, Staples is credited with revolutionizing and focusing the home-office category in Canada by providing consumers with one-stop shopping in big-box stores with plenty of parking.

Starbucks

With the exception of Wal-Mart, no U.S. category killer has made a bigger international splash than Starbucks, which has, as of this writing, almost two thousand locations in thirty-three markets outside North America, representing about 7 percent of its total revenues of almost $10 billion. The Seattle-based coffee giant has an ambitious goal of fifteen thousand stores in fifty markets outside North America by the end of 2005. Eventually, if all goes according to plan, Starbucks's overseas stores will outnumber its domestic stores. Considering that Starbucks did not open its first non–North American store until 1996, that is an impressive goal. It is also necessary because, as it matures, Starbucks will eventually run out of viable markets in the United States. It has become an efficient machine, with the capacity to design and open a store in sixteen weeks or less and to be able to recover its initial investment in thirty-six months. Starbucks could eventually challenge McDonald's (which operates almost thirty thousand company-owned restaurants and franchise locations around the world) as the world's biggest restaurant chain. Starbucks is shooting for at least twenty-five thousand company-owned and -licensed units both domestically and internationally. Clearly, overseas expansion is going to be the key driver.

Starbucks opened its first international café in 1996 in the stylish Ginza shopping district of Tokyo. It was a good place to start because Japan is the third-largest coffee-consuming country in the world (after the United States and Germany). In the 1960s, long before Starbucks arrived on the scene, the sophisticated Japanese coffee culture was centered in small coffee houses called *kissatens*, primarily mom-and-pop operations, which served small cups of coffee for under a dollar. In the 1970s and 1980s, patrons would come to play video games that were built into the tables. After reaching a peak of 150,000 to 200,000 stores in the 1980s, *kissatens* began losing their popularity. Today, there only about about eighty thousand to ninety thousand such establishments in Japan.

Starbucks in Japan was an immediate sensation. Starbucks (pronounced STAH-buks-zu) Coffee Japan Ltd. was formed as a joint venture with Sazaby, Inc., a Japanese company that operates upscale bakeries, restaurants (including tearooms called "Afternoon Tea"), and a chain of fashionable housewares stores, which are intended to attract their target audience—

women between the ages of twenty and thirty-five. Like its American counterparts, the Starbucks in Japan featured comfortable sofas and American music (initially hip-hop and reggae). Prior to the arrival of Starbucks, habitués of Japanese cafés were used to whiling away their time sipping coffee out of tiny cups in dimly lit shops. Starbucks stores did not allow smoking, a factor that some said would guarantee failure. On the contrary, the smoke-free atmosphere captivated younger, health-conscious Japanese women, who are the supreme arbiters of what's hot and what's not in the land of the rising sun.

In the first few years, the Japan experience was so positive that it established the template for Starbucks's international expansion. By 2000, the joint venture company had opened three hundred stores and earned its first profit—$11.7 million on sales of $242 million, more than double the financial performance of the previous year.[4] Buoyed by the rapid growth in Japan, Starbucks entered into a series of joint ventures as it expanded into Europe, the Pacific Rim, the Middle East, Mexico, and Central and South America.

The chain's first foray in to Europe began in 1998, when it acquired a small bustling London-based chain called Seattle Coffee Company (no relation to Seattle's Best Coffee or SBC), which was the brainchild of a young expatriate couple. A few short years later, Starbucks had 149 stores in London alone, and more than three hundred in the United Kingdom. Expansion soon followed into Switzerland, Austria, Germany, Greece, Spain, Indonesia, and on and on. By 2004, Starbucks was operating in thirty-three countries outside the United States, including its first retail location in France through a joint venture in France with Grupo Vips, the same company Starbucks partnered with in 2002 to open its Barcelona and Madrid locations in Spain.

But international expansion has hit some bumps in the road. Although by 2002, twenty-five of the top thirty Starbucks stores in the world were in Japan, including the Shibuya store, which is the busiest in the entire chain, Starbucks's Japanese operations began showing drooping sales because of increased competition from Starbucks's Seattle-based rival Tully's Coffee and the Japanese-based Doutour Coffee, both of which were adding stores throughout the country. Starbucks saw a decline in its average annual revenue per store—over $1 million each. Starbucks, which intends to have more than a thousand locations in Japan, began adding small kiosk-sized mini-versions in subway and train stations to catch the millions of commuters, similar to the little cafés that Starbucks tested successfully at Grand Central Terminal in Manhattan. By cutting costs and expanding its food menu, Starbucks was able to reverse its downward trend in Japan by the close of the fiscal year that ended on March 31, 2004.

Starbucks's international problems were not restricted to Japan. In 2002, the company had to buy out its partners in its distressed operations in Switzerland and Austria, closed six unprofitable cafés in Israel, and began pulling back on international expansion. Many of Starbucks overseas operations are either licensing agreements or joint ventures with local partners, a strategy that makes it easier for the company to enter a market and to tailor its operations there to local tastes and customs. The downside to those arrangements is that Starbucks's share of profits may be only 20 to 50 percent. There is speculation that Starbucks will readjust its joint-venture partnerships in order to get a bigger piece of the profits.

Starbucks, like other U.S. category killers, is also facing the challenge of copycats. In 1999, Doutor opened its Starbucks-like, smoke-free Excelsior Café, which has a layout and design so similar that it has been sued by the invaders from Seattle. The copycat situation is even more profound in China, where that type of emulative behavior is blatant and endemic. The Shanghai Xing Ba Ke coffee shops (loosely translated to "Shanghai Starbucks") apes the look and the logo of the American company, which has almost three dozen stores in Shanghai. Unlike

Starbucks, the Xing Ba Ke shops have waiters and higher-priced coffee drinks.

Such imitative moves are emblematic of what U.S. category killers face when they try to export their concepts overseas. In order to succeed, they must not only be better than their native competition, they must also be clever enough to overcome the inevitable obstacles placed in their path. International expansion will become increasingly important as category killers cope with the growing opposition in the United States, which we will explore in the following chapter.

PART III

The Winds of Change for Category Killers

8

The Backlash

Unless we can and do constantly seek and find
ways and means to do a better job; unless we accept the
challenge of the changing times; we have no right to
survive and we shall not survive.

—Chester O. Fischer

WITH TRADITIONAL department-store-anchored malls at
the end of their life cycle, mall owners and developers are living in the most difficult time in the past half-century to be
able to build a mall. Developable land near the desirable
demographics has become more scarce, and communities are
not greeting mall developers with the same kind of zeal that
they once did. In many areas, community groups are lining
up against developers, charging that whatever the new malls
might bring in by way of retail sales taxes, it will not compen-
sate for additional costs in infrastructure, police and fire pro-
tection, sprawl, air quality, and other quality-of-life-issues.
Mall developers have responded by trying to win favor
through contributions to local politicians and engaging in
public relations and lobbying campaigns. Working with commercial developers and acquiescent municipalities that thirst

for retail tax dollars, category killers use every available tool and strategy to expand their scope.

But these considerable efforts notwithstanding, over the past several years, big retail expansion efforts have been meeting with increasingly stiff opposition. Because of their high profile and far-reaching influence, category killers are often targeted by a broad cross-section of activists, including local and national grass-roots organizations, small business associations, guerrilla street-theater activists, consumer groups, populist politicians, and legal advocates ranging from libertarian to progressive. These groups have a variety of agendas, but the general thrust is to keep out—or to severely restrict—category killers and other big-box stores. This chapter discusses the problems—from logistical to ideological—facing these retailers.

Retail Redevelopment: Deep in the Heart of Taxes

What happens when you combine retailers and mall developers that desperately want to expand their size and scope, and elected officials that desperately need retail tax revenue for their cash-strapped municipalities? Two interest groups that need each other *desperately*.

It's no surprise that one of the fastest-growing membership segments of the International Conference of Shopping Centers trade association comprises public officials looking to devise retail projects that will renovate blighted neighborhoods, provide jobs and rejuvenate tax bases. Typical of the politicians that attended the ICSC convention in Las Vegas in 2003 was Rita L. Mullins, mayor of Palatine, Illinois, who told other delegates: "Give me retail or give my city the budget death knell."[1]

John Darby, a city councilman of Lacey, Washington, who voted to approve a Wal-Mart in his neighborhood, told the *Seattle Times*: "When the city of Lacey is projecting an operating deficit in 2006, do I think $500,000 in sales taxes a good thing? Absolutely."[2]

While many upscale suburban and urban communities have lined up against retailers and developers, there are also many communities—particularly in underserved, under-stored urban (read: minority) areas, that are welcoming big-box category killers with open arms.

"There seems to be an inverse relationship between the need for retailing in general and the opposition to it," noted Michael Beyard, a fellow with the Urban Land Institute in Washington, D.C.[3] "Cities that have been devastated by retailers moving out to suburban areas tend to be far more welcoming of the big box stores than those cities that have a vibrant retail sector. In cities where neighborhoods do not have retail services, we see that there is great support of city efforts to bring in the big-box stores simply because people are tired of driving so far to take advantage of the low prices that everyone else is getting. On the other hand, cities that have a large immigrant population, with thriving retail streets, tend to be much more wary of the big boxes because they will compete directly with those small mom-and-pop stores and drive them out of business."

Because many municipalities are funded largely by commercial taxes, Beyard calls it "irresponsible for cities to allow that drain of retail dollars to continue when they have opportunities to increase the amount of retail space of whatever type within their boundaries."

Category killers and other traditional brick-and-mortar retailers have been battling pure-play Internet retailers over the issue of collecting state sales taxes on Internet purchases. The U.S. Congress had initially taken a hands-off approach to collecting taxes on Internet sales because it did not want to stifle a new business channel. Online shoppers are required to pay sales taxes directly to their states, but they rarely do. At present, states are not allowed to compel the payment of taxes because the U.S. Supreme Court decided that collecting taxes by navigating through all the various state tax systems presented an inequitable hardship on retailers that do not have a physical presence (stores or warehouse) in the states where online customers live.

In 2003, in a move to try to level the playing field, a group of major retailers, led by Wal-Mart, Target, and Toys "R" Us, made a deal with thirty-eight states and the District of Columbia to have their online divisions collect sales tax. The assumption was that the agreement would give a boost to the states' drive to collect online sales taxes in general. Wal-Mart and Toys "R" Us claimed that they entered into the agreement so that their customers would be able to do in-store returns or exchanges of items they had bought online—a difficult task, because the sales tax issue muddied the waters. But a more compelling reason for those big chains to enter into the agreement was the fact that their online revenues are only a small part of their business. Consequently, paying individual state sales tax would constitute less of a burden on them than it would on operations like Amazon.com or eBay. Under the terms of the deal, the states agreed to absolve the stores of any liability for previously uncollected online sales taxes that they might have had to pay because they have operations in so many states.

State and local government agencies have been pushing a tax proposal called the Streamlined Sales Tax Project (SSTP), which is intended to overhaul the sales tax system. These government agencies claim that SSTP would establish uniform national standards for all types of commerce, both interstate and intrastate. One feature of SSTP changes the application of sales taxes to retail sales from the "point of sale" (the physical location where the shopper buys the product) to the "point of delivery" (where the shopper takes possession of the product). In other words, when a buyer takes possession of (in other words, picks up) merchandise at a store, that store is considered the point of delivery. But if the buyer orders the merchandise from a Web site or a catalog and that merchandise is delivered to her home, then her home is considered the point of delivery. Therefore, her home state is entitled to the sales tax. As of April 2004, twenty states have enacted all or part of the taxation legislation spelled out in the Streamlined Sales Tax Project.

But this law can also have adverse effects on municipalities like Tukwila, Washington, the home of all the stores in the Southcenter area (described in chapter 1). For example, if a shopper living in the adjacent town of Renton purchased a dining room set at one of the many furniture stores in Tukwila and had it delivered to her home, the local share of the tax on the dining room set would be collected by the city of Renton, not Tukwila. Therefore, Tukwila could potentially lose millions of dollars in sales taxes.

Eminent Domain

Eminent domain—the condemning and taking of private property by the government for public use—has become the nuclear weapon in competitive retail markets all across this country. Under the laws of eminent domain, the original owner of a piece of property must be awarded "just compensation" by the entity that takes the property, as spelled out in Amendment V of the Constitution of the United States. The original definition of "public use" included a project that obviously and directly contributed to the public good, such as the construction of highways, railroads, schools, and hospitals. But in the middle of the twentieth century, that definition took on, shall we say, a more *nuanced* interpretation.

The change began when the federal District of Columbia Redevelopment Act of 1945 created the Redevelopment Land Agency, which had, through eminent domain, the power to acquire real property as part of a program to improve inferior housing and blighted areas in Washington, D.C. Attorneys representing a Mr. Berman, the owner of a department store, argued that the government was barred from taking over his property through eminent domain because the Redevelopment Land Agency intended for it to be redeveloped for private—not public—use. The case eventually made it to the United States Supreme Court as *Berman v. Parker*. In a landmark 1954 decision, the Court expanded the definition of "public use" to embrace commercial development for "public purpose."[4]

Berman v. Parker enabled the District of Columbia to condemn the buildings in a run-down neighborhood so that condominiums could be built. The Court, with legendary liberal Associate Justice William O. Douglas writing the unanimous opinion, held that the redevelopment of the District of Columbia was a public purpose for which the United States could properly exercise its power of eminent domain: "The concept of the public welfare is broad and inclusive. The values it represents are spiritual as well as physical, aesthetic as well as monetary. It is within the power of the legislature to determine that the community should be beautiful as well as healthy, spacious as well as clean, well-balanced as well as carefully patrolled." Instead of "public use," the court believed that the more correct phrase should be "public interest" or "public welfare." The rationale was that condemnation served a higher "public purpose" than slums.

Berman v. Parker eventually paved the way for an even more directly and obviously business-oriented implementation of eminent domain in the Michigan Supreme Court's 1981 ruling in the case of *Poletown Neighborhood Council v. City of Detroit*. Back then, the Detroit Economic Development Corporation wanted to acquire a large tract of land in the Poletown neighborhood of Detroit so that General Motors could build an assembly plant. The city of Detroit was certainly invested in encouraging its largest employer to make new capital expenditures close to home. By a five-to-two majority, the Michigan Supreme Court bought the argument that justified the condemnation of private property and the transfer of that property to a private corporation to build a plant that would promote industry and commerce, and therefore add jobs and taxes to the economic base of the city and the state. Nevertheless, Justice James L. Ryan, who wrote the dissenting opinion in the case, was prescient about the slippery slope that his colleagues had just created:

> *"The Court has altered the law of eminent domain in this state in a most significant way and, in my view, seriously jeopardized the security of all private property ownership. This case will stand, above all else, despite the sound intentions of the majority, for judicial approval of municipal condemnation of private property for private use. This is more than an example of a hard case making bad law—it is, in the last analysis, good faith but unwarranted judicial imprimatur upon government action taken under the policy of the end justifying the means."* [5]

Ever since that decision was handed down in 1981, it has been cited in cases—in courts all over the country—that deal with the taking of homes and businesses for private business purposes. As a result, critics claim, eminent domain has been—and continues to be—abused by state, county and municipality government redevelopment agencies that work closely with private retailers and developers. In some cases, a city or agency will designate the area of a project and select a developer to assume the responsibilities for finding, selecting, and signing on the retail tenants.

"Cities love eminent domain because they can offer other people's property in order to lure or reward favored developers," writes Dana Berliner in her exhaustive study of the topic, *Public Power, Private Gain.* "Developers love eminent domain because they don't have to bother with negotiating for property. They can pick anywhere they want, rather than anywhere they can buy. And the compensation they have to pay is usually less than if they bought the property on the open market."[6]

The three most important criteria in retail are—and always will be—location, location, location. Because big-box retailers are interested in locations where thriving retail already exists, these are the areas that are generally targeted for appropriation through eminent domain.

Usually, the first step toward invoking eminent domain is to have a government entity declare an area as "blighted," which generally means physical deterioration. "Courts usually hold that using eminent domain to eradicate blight is for public use, whatever the eventual use of the property, because clearing away the blight is a benefit to the public," writes Berliner, an attorney with the Institute for Justice, a public-interest law firm in Washington, D.C. However, she cautions, there can be a wide interpretation of blight. "For example, a blighted area might have homes without electricity or plumbing, but it might also be an area that is 'economically under-utilized,' that has inadequate parking or 'inadequate planning,' or too-small yards. . . . Cities will even declare areas to be blighted that have no current blight but might be blighted in the future."[7]

After a property has been designated for eminent domain, it can be acquired for "fair market value" by the government entity overseeing the project. Unfortunately for sellers, they are not compensated for the good will that they have built up in their business over the years. (When a business is sold, good will generally is factored into the price that the buyer will pay for an ongoing, successful commercial concern.) Under the hammer of eminent domain, a property owner who chooses not to sell might very well face a condemnation lawsuit or might be the target of a "quick-take," whereby the government entity deposits with the court the monetary amount of what it estimates it would pay in compensation. While that's going on, the government can take possession of the property and be free to bulldoze it before the owner can have his day in court.

A popular technique for paying for these development projects is called *tax increment financing* (TIF). Generally, a city will earmark real estate taxes for its general fund in order to pay for city services or to guarantee outstanding municipal bonds. For new and larger projects, a city might use TIF, which is generated through the special assessment of property values by a local government that expects to benefit from the commercial or environmental improvement of the property. The increased (incremental) difference in tax revenues between the original assessment rate and the new, higher assessed rate is then used to pay for the improvement activity. Rather than finding their way into a government's general fund, the increased taxes are held by the development agency, which can then float debt without the need of a vote of taxpayers.

For example, an area is designated as a TIF district, effective January 2005. In 2004, let's say the area generated $100 in property taxes—every dollar of which went into the general fund. The following year, after TIF-back improvements, the same area generates $150 in property taxes. The additional $50 does not go into the general fund. Instead, it is earmarked for the coffers of the development agency, which has the option of using the money to fund the existing project, to repay the bonds that were initially issued for the project, or to direct those monies to fund additional development projects—depending on how the financing for the project was structured.

"Part of the reason that cities like Tax Increment Financing is that TIF enables the city or agency to capture dollars that would otherwise go to a different government body," Berliner told me. "There is a financial incentive on the part of the condemnor [the government agency that condemned the property] to try to capture those dollars. Even if it's not an increase for the government, it's an increase for the government agency."[8]

Since 1991, the Institute for Justice has been on the front-lines of the eminent domain wars, defending smaller business owners and private citizens whose property was taken by local governments and then turned over to retail chains and other private businesses. The Institute has been intimately involved in this issue since 1994, when New York developer Donald Trump wanted to expand his Trump Plaza Hotel & Casino in Atlantic City and install green space, a driveway, and space for special VIP limousine parking. To achieve Trump's plan, New Jersey's Casino Reinvestment Development Authority (CRDA) would have to buy several small businesses and a private home in the area. Some of the businesses agreed to sell; others didn't. The CRDA started condemnation proceedings against the parties that refused to sell. Ultimately, the local trial court ruled in favor of the small businesses.

Public Power, Private Gain details hundreds of similar examples of private companies using the power of government to exploit seized public property. Even the respectable New York Times Company was a beneficiary of eminent domain, thanks to Empire State Development Corporation (ESDC) a New York State so-called "public benefit" corporation that, according to its Web site, "provides financial and technical assistance to businesses, local governments and community-based not-for-profit corporations for economic development and large-scale real estate projects that create and/or retain jobs and reinvigorate distressed areas."[9] In 2001, at the company's behest, ESDC condemned ten businesses on the block between Seventh and Eighth Avenues and 40th and 41st Streets, the proposed site of the new headquarters for the "paper of record," which was also awarded many millions of dollars in tax breaks for building its headquarters near Times Square.

Another noteworthy case involving a category killer is that of Minic Custom Woodwork, a family-owned maker of high-end custom-made furniture and cabinetry. Founded in 1927, Minic had been operating out of the same location in New York's East Harlem neighborhood since 1979. The neighborhood was a mixed-use area of residences, small retail, and manufacturing. In 1981, the Minnich family bought the building they were operating in and spent more than a quarter-million dollars in renovations and permanent woodworking fixtures.

Minic was a highly respected company with a rich history. When owner William Minnich was a small child, Frank Lloyd Wright commissioned his father to construct models for a furniture line that the legendary architect had designed. (Some of those pieces are now in the permanent collection of the Metropolitan Museum of Art. Other Minic pieces have been exhibited in the Museum of Modern Art and the Brooklyn Museum.) The company also created wooden reindeer that were used in a scene in *Miracle on 34th Street*, the movie that tested people's belief in Santa Claus. But what happened to the Minnichs was proof that Kris Kringle had left Manhattan.

In 1998, Empire State Development Corporation wanted to redevelop the East Harlem neighborhood in upper Manhattan, an $87 million project on 116th Street and FDR Drive. East Harlem was located in a so-called "empowerment zone," which was set up to promote and encourage small businesses in the community. ESDC came up with a plan to condemn a dozen businesses, including the Minic Custom Woodwork building. It would then transfer the properties to Blumenfeld Development Group, one of New York's largest developers. Blumenfeld intended to create a commercial project called "East River Plaza." The centerpiece of the project would be a Home Depot store built on seven acres. It was announced that the store would employ an estimated four hundred people, most of them from the neighborhood, and that it would make shopping for home-improvement products more convenient for residents of Manhattan who previously had to travel to the suburbs or to other boroughs to shop Home Depot. Therefore, according to a Home Depot spokesperson, the store would "unquestionably" serve a public use. (Of course, there were already other local retailers that sold merchandise similar to that of Home Depot.) A Costco was also proposed for the site, covering five hundred thousand square feet of retail space, with the two anchors each occupying 120,000 square feet.

"The fact that there might be some incidental benefit to certain private individuals or private businesses doesn't undermine the overriding public purpose that we would be seeking to accomplish," said Joe Petillo, a lawyer for the ESDC.[10]

The Minnichs and many of their neighbors filed a lawsuit challenging the project. They were thwarted in both civil court and federal court because they had missed deadlines for appeal, which they claimed they were not aware of. Finally, after several years of legal wrangling, they gave up for personal and health reasons and ultimately sold their business to a competitor. They were also compensated by the developer. The Minnichs' story was picked up by several business publications, including *Fortune*, which drew increased attention to the potential for abuses in eminent domain cases.

Home Depot and Costco later pulled out of the project. As this book goes to press, the developers are still searching for anchor tenants for the project.

Free Enterprise for the Public Good?

Many big-box retailers find that being the beneficiaries of eminent domain is too good to resist. Costco, in particular, has been involved in several noteworthy eminent domain cases, particularly in California, where cash-strapped municipalities have long sought to balance their budgets with sales tax revenue generated by big-box stores.

Throughout the state, city officials claim that they have been restricted from raising revenue from other sources because, for the past decade, the state has been taking an increasingly greater share of local property taxes. The blame for this situation is pinned on the passage in 1978 of Proposition 13, which permanently decreased property tax rates on homes, businesses, and farms in California by about 57 percent. Proposition 13 amended the state constitution, which now specifies that property tax rates cannot exceed 1 percent of the property's market value, and that valuations can't grow by more than 2 percent per annum unless the property is sold. Proposition 13 also requires that all state tax rate increases be approved by a two-thirds vote of the legislature and that local tax rates have to be approved by a vote of the people. As a result, in order to generate taxes that will not find their way into the state coffers, California municipalities claim, they have no choice but to find ways to financially maximize all of their developable land, a plan of action that has been dubbed the "fiscalization of land use."

In 1998, in Lancaster, California, a 99 Cents Only discount store moved into a previously vacant space located adjacent to a Costco store in the Valley Central Shopping Center. A couple of years later, Costco wanted to expand its space in the shopping center. Although there was ample room on the other side, Costco wanted the space that was occupied by 99 Cents Only. Costco made rumblings that if they didn't get the 99 Cents Only space, they just might close their Lancaster store and move to Lancaster's bitter rival, neighboring Palmdale. Lancaster and Palmdale had battled for years to lure businesses away from each other, using incentives such as lower taxes and road improvements as their primary weapons, with each town trying to top the other.

Generating almost a half-million dollars in sales tax, Costco was the single largest financial contributor to Lancaster's $33 million budget. To illustrate how important were Costco's contributions to Lancaster's coffers, the city manager explained it this way: Taxes collected from Costco were enough to pay for all the city's recreation programs; they were enough to pay for all elective law enforcement operations, such as police stings.[11]

Faced with losing Costco, the city of Lancaster initiated eminent domain proceedings against 99 Cents Only, which responded by filing a suit to block the condemnation. On June 25, 2001, a federal district court ruled that the condemnation was not for public use. Judge Steven V. Wilson argued,

> *the evidence is clear beyond dispute that Lancaster's condemnation efforts rest on nothing more than the desire to achieve the naked transfer of property from one private party to another. Indeed, Lancaster itself admits that the only reason it enacted the [condemnation] was to satisfy the private expansion demands of Costco. It is equally undisputed that Costco could have easily expanded . . . onto adjacent property without displacing 99 Cents at all but refused to do so. Finally, by Lancaster's own admission, it was willing to go to any lengths—even so far as condemning commercially viable, unblighted real property— simply to keep Costco within the city's boundaries. In short, the very reason that Lancaster decided to condemn 99 Cents' leasehold interest was to appease Costco. Such conduct amounts to an unconstitutional taking for purely private purposes.[12]*

In March 2003, the U.S. Court of Appeals for the Ninth Circuit held that the case had become moot when Lancaster began building Costco another store. To keep Costco on its tax rolls, Lancaster gave the retailer almost five acres of the city's seventy-one-acre signature park and cleared the area by felling some hundred trees.

In another case, Costco's warehouse store annually contributes about $400,000 to the Cypress, California, city coffers.
Cypress is also the home of Cottonwood Christian Center, a
non-denominational church that had been trying for years to
develop an eighteen-acre tract that it owned into a new place of
worship, at a cost of about $50 million. The church claimed
that the bureaucracy of the city of Cypress had been slowing
down its efforts to acquire the proper permits. The reason for
the city's delays eventually became clear when the Cypress City
Council voted to create a redevelopment zone that would in-
corporate Cottonwood's tract, which was located at one of Cypress's busiest intersections near the Los Alamitos Race Track, a
popular facility for horse racing. The city wanted to develop
Cottonwood's property into a new retail development/town
center, to be anchored by a new Costco store. The city council
ordered a two-year moratorium on new developments within
the zone, ostensibly to enable it to more easily manage any
impending use of the property.

To get the church out of the way of development, in May
2002, the city council of Cypress actually had the church land
condemned under eminent domain, claiming it was located in
a "blighted" area—one of the conditions for eminent domain.
But in August of that year, a federal court granted the church an
injunction to stop the condemnation. Federal Judge David
Carter wrote: "The framers of the Constitution might be surprised to learn that the power of eminent domain was being
used to turn the property over to a private discount retail corporation." Regarding the designation of the property as blighted,
Judge Carter said: "Assuming that removing the blight from the
Cottonwood property was a compelling state interest, the city
could eliminate the blight simply by allowing Cottonwood to
build its church."[13]

In February 2003, Cottonwood agreed to swap its land for
another site nearby, thereby freeing the city of Cypress to
build its development.

WE CAN SEE a pattern here: In the end, it's easier to settle with an opponent with deeper pockets than you.

Although Wal-Mart and Home Depot also have been involved in their share of eminent domain cases, Costco's name continually pops up in such cases in places as varied as Lenexa, Kansas; Maplewood, Missouri; and Port Chester, New York. The company's zeal is understandable: It has become increasingly difficult for big-box stores like Costco to find in urbanized locations the necessary fifteen-acre tracts it requires to open a store. Costco publicly has admitted as much. In response to a letter from a shareholder who had raised the question of the strategy of eminent domain, the firm's chief legal officer responded, "There are probably dozens of . . . Costco projects where eminent domain or the threat of it has been involved in acquiring land for redevelopment."[14]

The combined self-interest of the big-box stores and needy city governments has upset the level playing field of free enterprise. This, in combination with quality of life factors, has contributed to a growing backlash, a call for these companies to be held more accountable to the communities they occupy.

Opposition Forces Versus Wal-Mart (and Others)

Wal-Mart is aggressively adding more SuperCenter stores, including some that are anchoring power center malls comprised of other big-box category killers. Each and every week Wal-Mart attracts in excess of seventy million people. At its current annual rate of growth of 15 percent, the retailer will double its size in five years, and chief executive officer Lee Scott believes that Wal-Mart could eventually be three times its present size. The growth will come from SuperCenters, which are shopping centers unto themselves, featuring everything from a dry cleaner to an optometrist under one roof.

With more than $4.5 billion in cash, the company can do pretty much anything it wants. "Wherever the Wal-Mart Super-Center goes, then the other big boxes follow. They want to go with the new kid on the block and form another bigger, second-generation center," said Malcolm R. Riley who develops power centers in California. "Wal-Mart's SuperCenters give them such an excellent return on investment. They know that this is the wave of the future. They are not going to let somebody else come along and build that machine. They are going to build it."[15]

For years, Wal-Mart has been engaged in its own creative destruction. The company thinks nothing of closing a successful 125,000-square-foot store that annually generates $50 million in sales and replacing it with 225,000-square-foot SuperCenter a mile or so down the road. The retailer has a division that does nothing but sell off excess properties. Wal-Mart is the country's biggest property developer, with 550 million square feet of selling space in 2002, according to Retail Maxim. Its portfolio of real estate comprises about *3 percent of the world's total retail space.*[16]

All told, in fiscal 2004, Wal-Mart will have added about fifty million square feet of retail space, a 9 percent increase over the previous year, when they added forty-six million square feet, another 9 percent jump. The U.S. expansion alone included fifty to fifty-five discount stores and 220 to 230 SuperCenters. About 140 of the SuperCenters will be relocated or expanded stores, with the balance constructed in new locations. Wal-Mart is increasingly opening stores in well-to-do suburbs such as Plano, Texas (outside of Dallas), and Alpharetta, Georgia (located near Atlanta). These stores carry merchandise—such as gourmet desserts and big-screen plasma TVs—designed to appeal to the upscale consumer. More than a thousand new SuperCenters will be open by 2008.

"There has never been a retailer that thinks the way that Wal-Mart does," said Riley. "They can't keep the stores they've got, so they are just closing them and building all new stores down the road. Theirs is an incredible strategy that's causing new power centers and new retail to be developed. In one case, we bought a building from Wal-Mart that I developed ten years ago, tore it down, and built a Home Depot. There is as much action and churning going on now as we've ever had, mainly because of this incredible machine called Wal-Mart."

On the positive side, many of the retail spaces abandoned by big-box stores are being developed by enterprising visionaries. For example, in the Dallas suburb of Irving, Texas, an Hispanic developer converted an 85,000-square-foot former Wal-Mart space into a Mexican-style market filled with more than a hundred merchants, several restaurants, a bingo parlor, a unisex barber shop, and a banquet room. One person's abandoned building is another person's opportunity. And there will be plenty of opportunities all across the United States. According to Marcus & Millichap, a national real estate investment brokerage company, 760 stores 75,000 square feet or larger were closed by major retail chains in 2002; 679 in 2003 and 191 through the first half of 2004.[17]

SHOULD WE ADMIRE WAL-MART?

Wal-Mart's many opponents are pursuing a strategy of a "death of a thousand cuts," the ancient Chinese phrase that describes the inflicting of numerous small wounds, none fatal in itself, but lethal in their cumulative result.

Although Wal-Mart is admired within the business community, as well as among a large portion of the shopping population, there is also no doubt that the retailer has become the most polarizing corporation in the United States. Newspapers and magazines have turned their sights on Wal-Mart, writing critical articles on the various lawsuits, community opposition, worker pay, and its alleged use of illegal-immigrant labor. *Fast Company's* December 2003 cover story was entitled "The Wal-Mart You Don't Know (Why low prices have a high cost)." The *Los Angeles Times* ran a series on Wal-Mart, including a story on its labor practices, entitled "Wal-Mart's empire reshaping workplace." The *New York Times* weighed in with "Wal-Mart, a Nation unto Itself." *Fortune* magazine, in its issue on America's Most Admired Companies of 2004, posed the question: "Should We Admire Wal-Mart?"[18]

No one is more aware of Wal-Mart's need to repair its image than the leaders of the corporation. Speaking to a meeting of analysts in September 2003, president and chief executive Lee Scott said that Wal-Mart was less concerned with "getting our detractors to love us," but rather to concentrate on "not creating the ammo that allows people to attack us. They attack us because they want to slow us as a company."

In 2001, Wal-Mart formed a task force to investigate how it is viewed by people both inside and outside the company. Wal-Mart is involved in national advertising and public relations campaigns intended to educate people on topics such as pay, advancement, and company benefits, and it has created a special office of diversity, which will develop a pool of qualified women and minority candidates. The company has even taken to underwriting programming on National Public Radio.

Obviously, at Wal-Mart's size, it will take a lot more than "a thousand cuts" to slow down this juggernaut. Ultimately, Wal-Mart's fate will be decided by American consumers, who will decide whether "every day low prices" at any cost—outweigh any other considerations, be they living wages, sex-discrimination allegations, or community aesthetics.

If no retailer pushes through as much development as Wal-Mart, no retailer stirs up more spirited opposition than Wal-Mart either, which every year faces dozens of challenges to proposed new stores. These challenges are among the biggest stumbling blocks in Wal-Mart's growth strategy, particularly as it hunts for new sites for its state-of-the-art SuperCenters.

Opponents argue that Wal-Mart and other big-box stores take away open space, create traffic and environmental problems, including air and water pollution, and contribute to the loss of small retailers and the death of downtown shopping venues. Some academic studies claim that Wal-Mart and other big-box stores don't bring in the level of sales and property taxes that justify their existence, and that taxpayers see little return for the taxpayer money, which county and state governments use to pay for improving highways and infrastructures for new big-box development, not community services. Studies in Mississippi and Iowa claim that Wal-Mart sales merely replace those that would have come from existing retailers.

In 2003, county supervisors in the San Francisco suburb of Contra Costa County passed an ordinance that bars a full-line grocery store from operating in nonincorporated portions of the county. The ordinance would also block any retailer larger than ninety thousand square feet from earmarking more than 5 percent of its floor space for food or other nontaxable goods. This legislation was intended to keep out Wal-Mart Super-Centers, which sell groceries at prices generally below those of unionized supermarkets. A similar resolution was enacted by the city council in Inglewood, near Los Angeles.

In early 2004, the citizens of Contra Costa voted to repeal the ordinance. Inglewood was a different story. In April of 2004, voters defeated a ballot measure that would have permitted the city to turn over to Wal-Mart a sixty-acre stretch of lifeless concrete near the Hollywood Park race track. The initiative would have essentially exempted Wal-Mart from virtually all state and local planning, zoning, and environmental regulations. In exchange, the retailer would have developed a shopping complex comprising a Wal-Mart SuperCenter and other chain retailers and restaurants. Despite desperately needing retailing, voters in this primarily African American– and Hispanic-dominated city defeated the measure by a 60-40 margin. A month later, at a contentious public meeting, the Chicago City Council gave zoning approval for Wal-Mart to build one store on the West Side of town (Wal-Mart's first unit in the Windy City), while voting against zoning changes for a store on the South Side.

In Palm Desert, California, three employees of the Safeway supermarket chain, who are members of the United Food and Commercial Workers Union (UFCW), filed a lawsuit against the city in order to delay construction of a SuperCenter, claiming in court documents that they would be "irreparably harmed by the approval of the project and its potentially detrimental environmental consequences."[19]

A similar suit—also over environmental issues—was filed in San Marcos, near San Diego, where the city council approved rezoning for a 139,000-square-foot SuperCenter. In March 2004, voters in San Marcos turned down Wal-Mart's attempt to open a second store there.

Wal-Mart suffered a stunning, unaccustomed setback in Dallas in 2002, when it made a full-bore attempt to gain approval for a prototype urban-focused SuperCenter near downtown, in the primarily upscale Love Field neighborhood, which includes affluent Highland Park as well as Oak Lawn, with its young, hip, gay population. With great fanfare, Wal-Mart had unveiled plans for the 204,000-square-foot store, which would comprise two stories on eleven acres of land—compared with its customary small-town, one-story building on twenty or more acres. The store was designed to

blend into the community with aesthetically inviting ele-
ments such as a Spanish tile roof, arched facade, decorative
windows and awnings, and picturesque gardens.

But the project was unanimously voted down by the Dallas Plan Commission, which called it an "oversized gorilla."
Although Wal-Mart redrew its plans *thirteen* times, it was still
rejected by a grass-roots coalition of neighborhood groups
that believed the store would overpower their community. It
was a rare defeat for Wal-Mart, whose heavy lobbying efforts
included donations to church organizations located near the
intended site.

In recent years, the opposition has been more effective—
and more clever and creative, using every tool at its disposal,
including environmental impact statements, restrictions on
design and store size, and the threatened withdrawal of subsidies. Community groups and grass-roots organizations are
fighting big-box stores in literally every corner of the United
States. For example, Homer, Alaska, a hamlet of 4,700 people
on the Kenai Peninsula, has capped the size of retail stores at
twenty thousand square feet in its central business district,
and forty thousand square feet in other commercial areas.
And in Vermont, the National Trust for Historic Preservation
placed the entire Green Mountain state on its annual list of
endangered sites because of the threat posed by big-box
stores, specifically Wal-Mart.[20]

Even in sprawling, uber-densely populated New Jersey,
then Governor James McGreevey declared a "war on sprawl,"
and ruminated about delaying the granting of water permits
for environmentally sensitive areas, restricting the construction of new highway access ramps, and creating "super
incentives" to attract developers to depressed cities such as
Camden, Newark, and Paterson.

McGreevey's efforts were part of a nationwide movement
toward so-called "smart growth," a system that was devised in
1999 with the backing of seven of the country's most influen-

tial philanthropic endowments: the Surdna Foundation, the Turner Foundation, The James Irvine Foundation, the Ford Foundation, the John D. and Catherine T. MacArthur Foundation, the David and Lucile Packard Foundation, and the Energy Foundation. Collectively called the Funders' Network for Smart Growth and Livable Communities, it seeks, according to its Web site, to "support and connect organizations working to advance social equity, create better economies, build livable communities, and protect and preserve natural resources."[21]

Another group involved in this movement is the Smart Growth Leadership Institute, which is affiliated with Smart Growth America, a Washington, D.C.–based advocacy group. Headed by former Maryland governor Parris Glendening, the leadership institute works with state and local elected officials to enact laws that would enable government and public entities to deal with "urban sprawl" by substituting measures associated with smart growth. Most of these initiatives have to do with employing the power of government to restrict growth.

Opposition to major chain retailers has been steadily growing in numbers and organization throughout the country, where there are local chapters of national organizations such as American Independent Business Alliance, the Business Alliance for Local Living Economies (an initiative of the non-profit Social Venture Network), the Institute for Local Self-Reliance, and Sprawlbusters. These groups work with local organizations such as the Salt Lake Vest Pocket Business Coalition in Utah, which pushes an agenda that is more friendly to small, independent businesses, and MADSET (Milford Alliance to Defeat Sprawl at Exit Ten), comprised of residents of Milford, Pennsylvania, who fought against a Home Depot.

The Salt Lake Vest Pocket Business Coalition is dedicated to avoiding becoming "Anywhere USA," according to the organization's president Peter Corroon. "When people come to a town, they don't remember going to Home Depot. They remember the little café or the small neighborhood clothing shop," said Corroon. "Our feeling is that neighborhood businesses create a sense of place. People feel more strongly about their neighborhoods and commit to keeping them viable and safe. When people started driving out to shopping centers, they lost that sense of place. Now, we're trying to get that back."[22]

Opposition forces are utilizing some of the same kinds of studies, hardball tactics, and public relations campaigns that category killers have used for years. For example, in Austin, Texas, in 2002, a coalition of former government officials, neighborhood association representatives, educators, and environmentalists thwarted a proposed Borders Books & Music superstore planned for the intersection of Sixth Street and Lamar Boulevard. According to a study commissioned by a local nonprofit group, local retailers returned 300 percent more to the economy than did chain stores. Two of the local retailers who paid for the study were BookPeople and Waterloo Records, who—surprise, surprise!—would have been directly and adversely affected by Borders.

The town of Bridgehampton, Long Island, has changed its zoning laws to successfully fight off Barnes & Noble's attempt to develop a new superstore on Montauk Highway, despite the fact that B&N Chairman Leonard Riggio has a home in that community.

The community of Excelsior, Minnesota, a resort town on Lake Minnetonka, about twenty miles west of Minneapolis, is justly proud of its amalgam of locally owned businesses. To keep things that way, the Excelsior Area Chamber of Commerce in 2002 launched an advertising campaign that boosted established local independent retailers and discouraged chains from opening new stores. The tagline for the print and billboard campaign was "Secede from Starbucks Nation." The line was used because, according to the creator of the campaign, "'Starbucks Nation' in recent years has come to symbolize uniformity and commercialization."[23]

Others seem to share that view. In 1999, when Seattle played host to the World Trade Organization, the city was overrun by a motley collection of demonstrators protesting everything from third-world debt to the endangerment of sea turtles. The activities of some of these demonstrators included throwing bricks through the windows of downtown Starbucks stores, then vandalizing and looting them.

In Seattle, at least, Starbucks has become an all-purpose target for the evils of the world. In 2001, after an unarmed African American man was shot dead by Seattle police, a protest group organized a demonstration in front of a Starbucks in a predominantly African American neighborhood. The protesting group explained that they were picketing—and urging a boycott of—Starbucks because they wanted the coffee company to address the question of economic justice. Ironically, just a few months earlier, Starbucks had been praised for opening that very store.

This group was joined by Friends of the Earth and the Organic Consumers Association, which had been targeting Starbucks for, among other things, refusing to guarantee that their products did not contain rBGH and other genetically engineered ingredients, for not brewing and seriously promoting fair-trade coffee, and for allowing low wages and unjust labor practices on the coffee plantations of their suppliers.

In fact, Starbucks has probably done more than any other corporation to help indigenous farmers in foreign countries earn fair prices for their beans. The company, which has a department of corporate social responsibility, has donated millions of dollars to coffee farmers in the developing world and has purchased millions of pounds of fair-trade coffee. (Starbucks works with groups that support the fair-trade movement, which tries to guarantee that indigenous farmers in coffee-growing countries are paid fair prices for their beans.) An activist for the Organic Consumers Association, based in

Little Marais, Minnesota, said that rather than going after a much larger consumer products company such as Kraft, whose thousands of products in grocery stores include much less earth-friendly coffee products, the group was singling Starbucks out because of its high visibility and because it attracts consumers with a social conscience.[24]

Back in Excelsior, Minnesota, the campaign opposing Star-bucks Nation included a series of "handwritten" letters to Starbucks (as well as to the Hard Rock Café and Home Depot). The epistle to Home Depot said: "Thank you for your interest in our fine lakefront town. . . . But with all due respect, we think we have it covered when it comes to home improve-ment. You see, we already have a few hardware stores of our own and even our own paint shop. . . . We know you have shelves stocked up to the ceiling. . . . But, no offense, you've never seen where we live. Chris at True Value has and knows exactly what we need."[25]

The negative reference to Starbucks is ironic because this is the company that did not displace existing business; rather, it literally invented the modern coffeehouse concept and made the world accept paying $4 for the same cup of Joe for which it once paid fifty cents. In the early 1990s, there were about two hundred coffeehouses in the United States (and probably not a one in Excelsior, Minnesota); today there are some fourteen thousand, according to the Specialty Cof-fee Association.[26] About 25 percent of these are Starbucks; the overwhelming majority are independent mom-and-pop operators brewing lattes and cappuccinos with hefty profit margins. As category creator and killer, Starbucks has edu-cated the market to both product and price, and given inde-pendent coffee shops the cover they need to occasionally raise their own prices.

Some efforts to slow down Starbucks are just plain silly. In San Francisco, the president of the Board of Supervisors expressed support for legislation that would require that people living within 150 feet of any proposed new drugstore or coffee shop be notified at least a month before a building permit could be issued. Even local retailers had a hard time with that one because they feared being trapped in bureaucratic red tape.

OTHER EFFORTS AGAINST big-box category killers are less community-focused and more amusing guerilla theater. Take Whirl-Mart Ritual Resistance. Activists who are part of this "resistance" wordlessly push empty shopping carts through the aisles of Wal-Mart and other big-box stores, utilizing "tactics of occupation and reclamation of private consumer-dominated space for the purpose of creating a symbolic spectacle," according to its Web site. Whirl-Mart was created by an activist named Andrew Lynn, who calls his anti-consumerism expression a "participatory experiment" comprised of "art and action." When store managers tell Lynn to protest somewhere else, he replies: "This isn't a protest. We're performing a consumption-awareness ritual." This "consumption-awareness ritual" has spread to dozens of cities, and aspiring ritualists can download a Whirl-Mart starter kit from Lynn's Web site.[27]

On the other hand, environmental activists have found that they can exploit the high-profile presence of category killers to their own advantage. For example, in 1999, a group called the Forest Stewardship Council, or FSC, pressured Home Depot to stop selling wood that came from endangered ancient forests and to substitute that supply with wood products that were certified by the FSC. Since then, the home-improvement retailer has worked with its suppliers and customers to phase out the use of endangered wood species. Today, Home Depot claims to know the source of 8,900 different wood products, including the blades on its ceiling fans.

Another environmental group, Forest Ethics, persuaded Staples to increase its inventory of recycled paper products in an effort to wean the office-products retailer from selling paper products from old-growth trees. Rival Office Depot, in a move to enhance its reputation as a "green" retailer, formed an alliance with several conservation groups to advance research into managing forests and protecting endangered species.

Declaration of Independents

Competent, creative independent retailers don't need to use resistance tactics in order to survive. These merchants understand that, to compete successfully, they must provide something that customers can't get anywhere else. To run a specialty store that successfully competes with category killers, you have to specialize to an even greater degree. If you own a garden store, you're not going to be able to sell impatiens as cheaply as Wal-Mart or Home Depot. So why not offer uncommon plants, or higher-end garden tools or ornaments?

Gregg Rosenberg is the co-owner of Beverly's Pet Center, which has two stores in South Florida, in Pembroke Pines and Coral Springs. Beverly's, a family-owned business that has been around since 1974, carries what one would expect in a pet store: dogs, cats, and reptiles, as well as ferrets and hedgehogs and a large selection of exotic hand-raised baby birds such as parrots, macaws, cockatoos, and other rare and hard-to-find species.

"Take out the livestock, and we have an 80 percent overlap in products with big-box stores," said Rosenberg. And there are plenty of those around. Beverly's stores are surrounded by the likes of PETsMART, PETCO, Pet Supermarket, and Pet Supplies Plus. In fact, a couple of years ago, there was a PETsMART location across the street. But PETsMART left the neighborhood and moved into another space a few miles away. Beverly's relocated into the abandoned PETsMART space, which doubled its square footage.

What separates Beverly's from other pet stores is its expertise in fish; the retailer claims to have the largest selection of fish and supplies in South Florida. If you want to buy a Zebra moray eel or a freshwater African cichlid (similar to an American sunfish) or build an aquarium from 2.5 to 225 gallons, and you live in South Florida, you'll probably find yourself at Beverly's.

Over the years, Pat Sullivan of Sullivan's Hardware, a four-store chain based in Indianapolis, has succeeded by carving out a niche in the higher end in certain categories, stocking brands known for their superior performance or quality. For example, Sullivan's carries the premium Porter Paint line, "which is a big deal around here," he said, for $30 to $35 a gallon. "Why bother selling the same thing that everyone else is selling?" he asked rhetorically.[28] "With wood stain products, I can't win the Thompson's Water Seal game," referring to a product that is sold through many retail outlets. Instead, he carries the premium, higher-priced SuperDeck deck stain, which provides a superior profit margin and sets Sullivan's apart from the Home Depots and Lowe's stores in the Indianapolis area.

Sullivan also shops his competition to find product categories that are not particularly price-sensitive, such as basic tool kits and paint accessories, which give him an opportunity to make a better profit. Sullivan remarked, "We have to compete on price; customers won't pay more."

Small, independent booksellers are another category of retailers that need to find a niche if they hope to survive. Ever since the advent of the Barnes & Noble and Borders superstores, membership in the American Booksellers Association, the organization that represents independent booksellers, has steadily dwindled, from 5,200 in the early nineties to some 1,850 today.[29] In the late 1990s, the ABA filed a federal lawsuit against Barnes & Noble and Borders, alleging that the chains used their buying power to get better—and allegedly illegal—deals from publishers, such as cash discounts and better credit terms. The suit was eventually settled out of court, but whatever the result, independents that have not clearly established a reason for being will continue to be on the endangered retailer list.

The problem with many small independents is that they got into the business because they loved books—not necessarily because they loved *selling* books. One bookseller who both loves books and loves selling books in a creative way is Collette Morgan, co-owner, with her husband Tom Braun, of the children's bookstore Wild Rumpus Books in Minneapolis. In 1992, Morgan, a veteran of the book business, decided to open a store that would be "something a corporate mind would never dream up and that a large company could never sustain; a place that would sell children a good time along with their reading material."[30]

Morgan is often asked to speak to fellow owners of small bookstores. "I tell them to stop bitching and complaining and get out there and do something different. Too many of them want to do things the same way as the big-box stores; then they're dead in the water. We do things they can't do or wouldn't dream of doing. B&N guys in suits would come into the stores with clipboards taking notes. They were obviously trying to copy things that we were doing but they couldn't pull it off. They are too corporate minded. We try to do the opposite of what a B&N would do."

Wild Rumpus is two thousand square feet of bookstore—and zoo. While borrowing its name from a phrase in Maurice Sendak's book *Where the Wild Things Are* (the character of Max declares "Let the wild rumpus start"), the store design was inspired by Anne Mazer's *The Salamander Room*, in which a boy transfigures his bedroom into a place where his salamander would be comfortable. The lad gradually brings into his room trees, frogs, and birds, and opens up the roof to the sky.

The front of the store conjures up images of an English neighborhood bookstore. The front door of Wild Rumpus is really a door-within-a-door—one for big people and a four-foot-high purple door for little people. The ceiling opens to expose the sky above the garden. Children can settle into a little shed where they can curl up to read scary books. Resident animals are all over the store: four cats and two chickens (Dalai and Elvis) roam the floors; a half-dozen occupied bird cages are scattered throughout the store; gray rats are confined to a clear Plexiglas-covered cage, which doubles as the creaky floor of the Haunted Shack, where little boys come to play and to watch the rodent entertainment. Separately caged tarantulas and ferrets hang out by the counter. An aquarium of fish can been found in the bathroom behind the one-way mirror, so that they can only be seen in the dark.

By creating an inviting place, Morgan has found a way to create traffic and make Wild Rumpus a destination store in the urban Linden Hills neighborhood of south Minneapolis, where, within ten miles, there are six Barnes & Noble stores, three Borders, a Target, and a Musicland. On Saturday afternoons, Wild Rumpus regularly hosts a wide variety of typically quirky in-store events to attract its loyal audience of young customers. Drop in some Saturday, and you might see the shearing of a sheep, and a display of books on how to raise sheep or how to card and dye wool or how to knit.

A Part of the Community

Category killers are forever trying to be part of the community and to show that they are being good neighbors and corporate citizens. The big boxes can do this to some extent, working with local groups on community clean-ups or sponsorships. But small independent stores can also do this because they are truly a part of the community.

Wild Rumpus works closely with community organizations. "We would rather devote our energies to community outreach, rather than opening up another storefront location," said Morgan. The store has had a long-standing association with local pediatricians, selling them the children's books that are available in their offices. Learning that schools in the Twin Cities were increasing courses in French classes, she increased the number of French-English titles available in the store.

Pat Sullivan has been giving home improvement and gardening advice to the community on his local weekend radio program for almost a decade. When he began his show in the mid-1990s, it coincided with the arrival of Lowe's and Home Depot in the market. These days, he's on every Saturday from 11 A.M. to 1 P.M. with a home-improvement show, and Sundays, 8 A.M. to 10 A.M. with a home and garden program.

"The radio program has helped us grow our business and solidify ourselves in the community," he said. "It's much easier to open a store when you have instant name recognition. And when customers come in the store and find out that I'm the one who's waiting on them, they can't believe I'm actually working. I don't ask my employees to do anything I that I'm not willing to do myself. When they do see me work, they see that this place is for real."

In 1994, a store opened up in a 1,500-square-foot space in the business district of my neighborhood in West Seattle. It had an odd name—"Quidnunc," which is Latin for "What now?"—and an odd mission: to sell computer software. When I first saw the store, I thought that whoever came up with this idea was either brilliant or bonkers—after all, category killers such as CompUSA, Computer City (now deceased), Office Max, and Office Depot were just a few miles away.

But timing is everything. There were a lot of things happening at that time in the world of computers. "It was the early days of the Internet, so I helped people learn how to get online," said founder and owner Bill Hibler, who also offered lessons for people who wanted to learn the intricacies of MS-DOS and Microsoft Word.[31] Soon after, he began carrying printer ink cartridges and cables. Eventually, he enlarged his space and hired technicians who build and repair computers. In 2002, he moved to a bigger space in the same neighborhood, on the main shopping street in West Seattle. I remain a loyal customer. The staff has built two computers for me, they are my Internet Service Provider and they host my Web site. It's not just a store, but also a community resource. That's how a small specialty business competes: by being *special*.

OPPOSITION TO BIG-BOX STORES has been building, both at home and abroad. The battle has been heating up for years, as powerful forces take sides. How category killers and Wal-Mart deal with their opponents will determine not only their future, but also the future of retailing. But while communities, churches, independent retailers, ad hoc committees, and anti-consumerists have every right to fight tooth-and-nail against category killers and other big-box stores, they must also provide a positive alternative that works for the community. Creativity must not be limited to clever means of protest; it must be extended to offering great solutions that help forge loyal customers. That is the only sure-fire way for independent retailers to survive in the world of category killers.

9

The Changing Shape
of Retail

You can never plan for the future by the past.

—Edmund Burke

WHAT IS THE FUTURE of category killers? Where will they turn up next? And how will they influence—and be influenced by—the changes in America's consumer culture? One thing is for certain: category killers will have to find their place—literally and figuratively—in the ever-shifting landscape of retailing in the twenty-first century, which is influenced by changing demographics, migration, shopping malls, and community and consumer needs.

A Shifting Landscape

As David Brooks points out in his book *On Paradise Drive: How We Live Now (And Always Have) in the Future Tense*, "We're living in the age of the great dispersal," as Americans are migrating "from the inner suburbs to the outer suburbs, to the suburbs or suburbia,"[1] building veritably instant communities in places like Mesa, Arizona (near Phoenix) and Pahrump, Nevada (near Las Vegas). We are seeing farmland and wilderness becoming exurbs (suburbs of suburbs) and suburbs becoming urbanized. In 2002, about 14.2 percent of Americans pulled up stakes and moved elsewhere. A significant portion of our peripatetic population is not tied to a job, a factory town, or other traditional reasons for staying put.

This longing for something new over the horizon (or down in the valley or across the river) has had a major influence on the retail stores that will sell to, and serve the American consumer. Category killers and big-box stores are a bit like the eighteenth-century itinerant peddlers who traveled America to seek customers for their wares. When faced with population shifts, category killers are more than happy to abandon one location and to quickly build another one a mile or two down the road.

At no time in American history have we seen such an ever-changing retail landscape, where old sites are abandoned and new opportunities arise at breathtaking speed. David Brooks describes it like this: "It's as if Zeus came down and started plopping vast development in the middle of farmland and the desert overnight. . . . A big box mall. Boom!"[2]

And that's just in recently developed parts of the country. What about all that land currently occupied by existing malls? Consider all of the old mall real estate that is coming on line. Since the mid-1990s, at least three hundred older shopping malls have been leveled, shut down, or converted to an alternative use, according to the Urban Land Institute; an additional three hundred to five hundred regional malls are destined for a similar fate over the next few years. Urban planners refer to these developed retail properties as "greyfield" malls whose survival requires the assistance of both the public and private sectors. Greyfields fall between "brownfields," which are abandoned, inactive or underused sites that may be contaminated (e.g., gas stations), and "greenfields," which are undeveloped suburban or rural properties. These regional centers cover about thirty or so acres and 300,000 to 400,000 square feet of retail space, and traditionally have been anchored by at least one large full-line department store. The most viable of these regional centers are being expanded to super-regional centers, covering fifty or more acres with 750,000 to 2,450,000 square feet of retail space, anchored by several large full-line department stores, who will have survived the consolidation in the department store sector. In order to respond to increased competition in the marketplace, more than 60 percent of these centers have undergone renovation and/or expansion in the past five years, According to the International Council of Shopping Centers.

No wonder the Los Angeles Forum for Architecture and Urban Design once held a "Dead Malls Competition" as a forum for generating new thinking on how to alter the traditional shopping mall. This contemporary direction in real estate development is a part of an urban design movement called "New Urbanism," which is dedicated to creating mixed-use neighborhoods where people can live, work, shop, and recreate, in spaces within walking distance of their homes. Developers and retailers are currently trying to figure out how to define the mall and how to keep viable the existing retail real estate.[3]

"Most communities don't realize the enormous real estate opportunity they have," says Michael Beyard of the Urban Land Institute.[4] "These older retail areas need to rethink what they are. They should be torn down and replaced by something new. There should be rezoning for housing, etc. Less than 25 percent of the U.S. population is in a family unit under one roof with a child. This is a generational shift that is as important as the introduction of the regional shopping mall."

Westfield Holdings Limited, the Australian-based shopping center developer (which owns the Southcenter mall), believes that—with the consolidation of department stores—

mall developers must assemble in one center every kind of retailer: category killers, department stores, general merchandise discounters, warehouse clubs, and supermarkets, as well as movie theaters and restaurants. Although common in Europe and Australia, this kind of hybrid center is only just beginning to be seen in the United States.

"Historically, the department stores didn't want the discounters in their malls, so the discounters went across the street," said Richard Green, vice-chairman of Westfield Holdings.[5] "Today, companies like May, Nordstrom, Sears, and Macy's see that it's good to have a Target or a Wal-Mart in the same mall because those stores create more traffic. The center of the twenty-first century is orienting itself to having many types of retailers under one roof—from Costco to Neiman Marcus and everything in between. That's why we believe that a lot of the retail real estate that some people thought was going to be dead is going to be vibrant."

Many malls that were once enclosed are being converted to open-air formats. These properties are being split up for easier access, adding many more points of entry as they combine the outdoor open strip mall with the supercenter concept to produce the feel of a community center. In this type of arrangement, retailers will be able to attract customer traffic from the streets, not just from within the mall. Faced with the problems of vehicle traffic, air quality, and urban sprawl, developers are taking unused or underused parts of their malls and creating mixed-use, pedestrian-friendly spaces that combine residential, office, and retail space, as well as a variety of urban services, such as medical care, and libraries, post offices, and other government buildings. Places such as Reston Town Center outside of Washington, D.C., and Town Center Drive in Valencia, California (thirty miles north of downtown Los Angeles) are attracting people who prefer to live close to where they work and to have all the amenities they need close by. Some malls are adding hospitals, churches, and daycare centers. Others are bringing in barbershops, dry cleaners, drug stores and super-markets. Sounds very much like the old Main Street (as well as the first shopping centers built in the 1940s and 1950s), but with a modern twist.

This type of scenario has been appearing in places such as Maple Grove, Minnesota, and White Marsh, Maryland, which never grew around a central business district; and in major met-ropolitan areas such as Raleigh, North Carolina, with its Triangle Town Center, comprising a 1.3-million-square-foot enclosed regional center anchored by Dillard's, Hecht's, Hudson Belk, Sears, and Saks Fifth Avenue, and a neighboring outdoor space called Triangle Town Commons, with a variety of shops and restaurants. In a formerly enclosed center in Sherman Oaks, Cal-ifornia, the roof has been removed, and what was once the Robinsons-May department store is now Warner Bros. Anima-tion Studios. The Villa Italia mall in the Denver suburb of Lake-wood has been transformed into a mixed-use development called Belmar, which includes retail and office space, as well as 1,300 residences in a variety of housing categories, and buildings that have entrances that face the street. In Chattanooga, Ten-nessee, Eastgate Mall, which was built in 1962, was redeveloped as part of an effort to breathe new life into the older suburb of Brainerd. The project was a joint effort of public and private interests. The mall property was reconfigured and reconnected with the surrounding neighborhood and an office park, and a new town square was constructed on the site of the mall's for-mer parking lot. The mall, in essence, was turned inside-out.

In many parts of the country, the old downtown center is coming back as aging empty-nest baby boomers return to the inner city so that they can shop and work within easy walk-ing or driving distance. The 1990 census showed a slight in-crease in inner city population for the first time since 1940; the 2000 census also showed a similar uptick. Because more and more consumers are interested in shopping within their own neighborhoods, local independent retailers are filling that need. One example is Birmingham, Michigan, whose bustling downtown retail core was threatened by the arrival of the 180-store Somerset Collection, a high-end mall in nearby Troy, which drew customers away, thanks to anchors Nordstrom, Marshall Field, Neiman Marcus, and Saks Fifth Avenue. Birmingham, the most affluent community in moneyed Oakland County, responded by creating a master plan to revitalize its upscale, pedestrian-friendly downtown by creating a mixture of residential, office, and retail space. Birmingham and many other smaller cities are working with single developers to create a master plan for their downtown shopping district that includes dining, entertainment, and multilevel shopping, provided by both national and local retailers. They take advantage of their size and neighborhood feel by sponsoring events, promotions and community activities to bring people downtown.

Over the past few years, a new retail concept—*lifestyle centers*—has burst upon the scene. The California development firm of Poag & McEwen is credited with creating the concept and registering the name "lifestyle center"—a free-standing upscale shopping environment that combines desirable specialty retailers and classic and contemporary architecture and landscaping with the convenience of a strip mall. The Shops at Saddle Creek in the Germantown area of Memphis, developed in 1987 by Poag & McEwen, is considered the first lifestyle center. These centers are ideally between 250,000 and 300,000 square feet, open air, with nearby parking.

Lifestyle centers and other smaller shopping concepts are a reaction to the need of time-pressed consumers to drive up to the store, get what they need and get out. They combine that quick-and-dirty in-and-out shopping experience with a little bit of Main Street, with cozy village squares and tree-filled parks, with a little bit of the upscale shopping experience of Rodeo Drive in Beverly Hills or the Magnificent Mile on Chicago's Michigan Avenue. They typically include tenants such as Talbots, Williams-Sonoma, and Barnes & Noble, as well as movie theaters and restaurants. There are more than a hundred lifestyle centers in the United States, with gross leasable space of about thirty-three million square feet. Between 2004 and 2006, the U.S. will add about 60 new lifestyle centers, which are usually situated in upscale neighborhoods with household incomes of at least $75,000.[6]

The Southcenter Example

Meanwhile, back in Tukwila, Washington, Westfield Holdings has big plans for the Southcenter mall, which it acquired in 2002 and renamed Westfield Shoppingtown Southcenter. Westfield, which owns a controlling interest in more than sixty U.S. shopping centers, will be adding to the mall's south side some 450,000 square feet of retail space, including large and small specialty stores, discounters, restaurants, and a sixteen-screen movie complex, thereby increasing the size of the Puget Sound area's largest regional shopping center to two million square feet. Most of the expansion is to be built on a former parking lot and six acres on a corner of Southcenter Parkway, where a hotel once sat. Further on down the road, a plot of land that once held a J.C. Penney distribution center and a single-story office building is also earmarked for retail expansion.

All told, the city of Tukwila, where all of this retail is located, collects about $1.6 billion in retail taxes, according to Alan Doerschel, finance director for the city; $15.6 million of that goes into the city coffers. But, as Doerschel points out, that money comes with responsibilities and obligations. "People think of Tukwila as a wealthy city because we have so few citizens (seventeen thousand) and all this revenue. We have to provide a huge amount of infrastructure and support to this commercial area. We need to keep the arterial streets open to keep traffic moving. We have seventy police officers; a town our size should have ten or fifteen. We have four fire stations; again, a town our size should have one fire station."[7]

Clearly, municipalities such as Tukwila and neighboring Renton (home of Wal-Mart, Ikea, and Fry's Electronics) have learned that there is no free lunch when it comes to the taxes generated by retail sales. All municipalities and local government entities must take these added responsibilities into consideration when they avidly recruit big-box retailers.

The Wal-Mart Effect

As we ponder the future viability of category killers, we must always keep in mind the overwhelming, unprecedented influence of Wal-Mart, the 800-pound gorilla that never leaves the room.

Wal-Mart has an impact on virtually every retailer and every retail category. Name a leading manufacturer of branded merchandise and chances are Wal-Mart is its biggest customer. The list is a who's who of consumer goods in the U.S.: Procter & Gamble, Kraft, Revlon, Gillette—to name a few. Wal-Mart's share of the total sales of consumer products companies is astounding: 28 percent of Dial's, 24 percent of Del Monte Foods', and 23 percent each of Clorox's and Revlon's. Wal-Mart moves more groceries, dog food, toys, socks, guns, apparel, detergent, jewelry, bedding, diamonds, furniture, toothpaste, sporting goods, CDs, DVDs, and videogames than any other retailer worldwide. It generates the most revenue for DVD releases of Hollywood movies, develops the most camera film, and fills more eyeglass prescriptions. Oh, yes, Wal-Mart is also the world's leading operator of private trucks, the biggest consumer of energy, and the largest developer of commercial real estate.

Thanks to Wal-Mart, Toys "R" Us, America's first category killer, is very much on the ropes. In 1998, Toys "R" Us lost

$132 million and was dethroned as the top toy retailer by Wal-Mart, which owns 21 percent of the domestic toy market, compared with Toys "R" Us's 17 percent share. (Target is next with about 9 percent, while Kmart and KB Toys each have 4 to 5 percent.) Wal-Mart, Target, and Kmart have the flexibility to increase their toy selection during the holiday season (thereby attracting more customers) and then return to normal levels the rest of the year. The discounters, with their more efficient pricing structure, can sell toys more cheaply than Toys "R" Us, which has gone through several management changes after Charles Lazarus retired as chief executive officer in 1994.

In 2000, John Eyler, the former chief executive officer of FAO Schwartz, the specialty toy retailer (which filed for Chapter 11 bankruptcy in 2003), took over as CEO of Toys "R" Us and began initiatives to improve customer service, store layouts, and ambience—to give the stores less of a warehouse feel. "All of retail has become more theatrical," said Eyler. "It's about making it fun. What's fun about going to a warehouse?"[8]

To spectacularly illustrate Eyler's point, Toys "R" Us spent some $35 million to construct what it claims is the world's largest toy store, in the heart of Manhattan at Times Square, on Broadway between 44th and 45th Streets. The four-level, 110,000-square-foot store makes a dramatic statement at the "Crossroads to the World." It is a multimedia center to introduce, launch, and showcase new products, and to sell the Toys "R" Us concepts of merchandising, rather than just boxes of toys and games.

The Times Square store features a wide variety of attractions not seen anywhere else. In the center of the four-story atrium is a sixty-foot-high Ferris wheel ride. Each of the fourteen cars on the Ferris wheel promotes a toy or character, such as Barbie or a Tonka Truck. A thirty-foot high, five-ton animatronic T. Rex dinosaur looks like it just left the set of *Jurassic Park*.

In this store, Barbie and her friends get to live in a two-story, four-thousand-square-foot Barbie mansion (complete with its own elevator), while King Kong stands atop a twenty-five-foot-tall replica of the Empire State Building. A life-size version of the Candy Land board game doubles as a candy store. A thirty-foot-tall glass wall that looks out onto Broadway catches the attention of passersby with special scrolling technology that transforms a window to a billboard (or vice versa) in just three seconds. There are personal shoppers for the truly serious toy consumers. VIPs can park themselves in a skybox balcony to view the never-ending activity. Some seven hundred employees roam this indoor theme park, while product demonstrations are going on as far as the eye can see and commercials continue to hype the merchandise from forty-five video monitors scattered at every turn.

All very nice, but that store didn't prevent 2003 from becoming the retailer's third disappointing holiday season in a row, and the worst since Eyler was hired. Same-store sales dropped by 5 percent. In 2004, Toys "R" Us closed 146 Kids "R" Us children's clothing stores and thirty-six Imaginarium stores, accounting for 11 percent of its total of 1,629 stores worldwide. Office Depot acquired 124 of the 146 the former Kids "R" Us stores for $197 million in cash, with plans to convert fifty or so to Office Depot stores. PETCO later bought twenty of those locations from Office Depot for their own stores

On the positive side, the company has done very well internationally; it holds a stake in the publicly traded Toys "R" Us Japan and also significant real-estate holdings. And it has a real winner in Babies "R" Us, its fastest growing and best performing domestic division, generating about 15 percent of the company's sales from its nearly two hundred stores. One of the advantages of the Babies division is that it stays busy all year round, as opposed to the Toys division, which relies heavily on holiday shopping.

The fate of this pioneering category killer will be uncertain as long as it relies on any one category—a category that Wal-Mart can dominate any time it wants to. Toys "R" Us, which once killed the small toy shop, is itself in the process of being, if not killed, at least seriously injured. As proof, in August 2004, Toys "R" Us announced that it may abandon the toy business entirely, selling its 1,200 stores to concentrate on Babies "R" Us (which itself might eventually be killed by Wal-Mart and Target).

Wal-Mart is exerting a similar impact on the home electronics business, particularly in areas such as service and pricing. Consumer electronics has become a low-priced commodity business, so that it is difficult even for specialty stores to make much in the way of sustained profits. A DVD player, for example, is familiar to most consumers, so discounters such as Wal-Mart and Target can pile them high and sell them cheap without having to hire knowledgeable sales and service help. Manufacturers put as much product information as possible on their Web sites (as well as the boxes the products come in), so that the customer is given enough data to make an informed decision, regardless of whether the purchase is ultimately made at Costco or Wal-Mart or Best Buy. Best Buy has yet to make significant inroads in home appliances, such as refrigerators, ovens, and microwaves—a category that is being aggressively earmarked by Lowe's and Home Depot, as well as Sears, the long-time leader.

Changing of the Guard

Inevitably, the entrepreneurial founders and leaders of now-mature category killers are being replaced by professional managers. This has happened in 2003 at Bed Bath & Beyond, where Steven H. Temares became CEO of the household-goods retailer, replacing co-founders Warren Eisenberg and

Leonard Feinstein, who remain as co-chairmen. In 2000, Orin Smith was named CEO of Starbucks Coffee, with Howard Schultz retaining the title of chairman and adding the title of "chief global strategist"; that same year, Eyler took over the helm at Toys "R" Us. In 2002, Bradbury Anderson became CEO of Best Buy; and Ronald Sargent assumed the chief executive position at Staples. In 2005, Robert A. Niblock will succeed Robert L. Tillman as chairman and CEO of Lowe's. Tillman had been at Lowe's for forty-one years, beginning as an office-manager trainee. It will be interesting to see if Niblock, whose background is in accounting, has the soul of a merchant.

The highest profile change was at Home Depot, the biggest of all the category killers. In 2000, founders Marcus and Blank were smart enough to recognize that it was time to bring in someone who knew how to manage a $60 billion–plus company. The Home Depot board surprised a lot of observers with the selection of Robert L. Nardelli as chief executive—making him the first executive without retailing experience ever to become CEO of a major nonfood retailer. A twenty-seven-year veteran of General Electric, and a disciple of GE Chairman Jack Welch, Nardelli had last worked at GE Power Systems, running lighting and power-generation plants. He was thoroughly schooled in GE's legendarily high-structured management culture, whose hallmarks are efficiency and discipline.

Efficiency and discipline were *not* the hallmarks of Home Depot, which reveled in a free-wheeling, entrepreneurial culture that attracted independent-thinking managers and employees who "bleed orange" (the company's signature color). After all, this was a company led by the inspirational Bernie Marcus, who once answered complaints from store managers about too much paperwork from the main office by telling them to "Get a rubber stamp that says 'Bullshit' on it, stamp it, and send it back to whatever bureaucrat sent it to you." In their 1999 book, Marcus and Blank wrote, "We hire people who couldn't work for anybody else, who might otherwise be well-suited to being self-employed or running their own shop, and many of them become store managers."[9]

That kind of attitude worked for Marcus and Blank, but not for Nardelli, who put an end to Home Depot's decentralized operation, which encouraged a culture in which many of the decisions were made at the store and regional levels. Nardelli folded ten regional buying offices into one centralized purchasing office to make the retailer more efficient, to increase its negotiating leverage with its vendors, and to get a better handle on inventory. With buying now centralized, Nardelli found a lot of redundancy of items in inventory, such as too many round-point shovels.[10] While regional managers were given greater accountability, virtually all decisions on purchasing came out of the headquarters in Atlanta. Take-charge store managers were no longer empowered to order whatever they needed for their store, whenever they needed it. This go-get-'em culture was similar to that of Nordstrom in its go-go growth years of the 1980s and 1990s, when store managers—and even some people on the sales floor—could order goods directly from the vendor. But as the Seattle-based retailer added more stores and hired more people to work in those stores, it couldn't get a tight control on its inventory. The trick was to control inventory without totally changing the culture. Home Depot employees had to deal with a similar shift.

To neutralize Home Depot's "cowboy" culture, Nardelli brought in from the outside a new corps of executives and managers—some from the military—who carried out the more disciplined plan of attack. Not surprisingly, Nardelli, who had the backing of the board, ruffled a lot of feathers among the old-timers, who felt he didn't understand their entrepreneurial culture. But with Lowe's applying significant competitive pressure, Home Depot had to make some changes—including painful ones. Wall Street, initially, was not pleased. Home Depot was the worst-performing stock in the Dow during 2002, losing 53 percent of its value, experiencing its first-ever overall sales decline. But by the end of 2003 and early 2004, Home Depot—greatly benefiting from the roaring real-estate market that propelled the sales of home-improvement products—was back on track. In fiscal 2003, sales rose 11 percent to $64.8 billion, and the company ended that year with several billion dollars in cash.[11]

Still, Nardelli and company will continue to be faced with the chronic problem of where Home Depot will be able to find growth after it has saturated the United States with its stores. In May 2004, in an effort to extend its reach to commercial builders and tradesmen, Home Depot acquired White Cap Construction Supply Inc., a seventy-store chain that sells a wide variety of professional building products, including industrial-grade tools, jackhammers and other construction equipment, and concrete-foundation forms. A few years ago, Home Depot had tried to lure home builders and contractors with a retail concept called "Home Depot Supply," but the idea didn't catch fire.

Indeed, all category killers will have to find other ways to expand, including creating new or small store concepts, exploring international markets, or acquiring other businesses. That last direction is the trickiest because most large retailers are finding it difficult to run more than one retail concept not related to their core business. That's why J.C. Penney unloaded its Eckerd drug store chain, and why Target sold its 62-unit Marshall Field department stores to May Department Stores Co., and put on the selling block its 266 Mervyn's discount apparel stores. Even Wal-Mart has not been able to make Sam's Club the equal of Costco.

Help Wanted

At a meeting of the International Mass Retail Association, executives of category killers and other big-box stores were asked to name their greatest business concern. Their answer:

hiring people. By 2010, there will be five hundred thousand more retail jobs than there will be people to fill them, according to the National Retail Federation. Consequently, retailers will have to pay more attention to retaining their best workers, so there will be more competition among retailers for sales associates. This is going to be especially challenging at a time when entry-level retail jobs are viewed as low-paying, dead-end positions. How are category killers going to find and keep good people by paying them a living wage at the same time that they are selling products at low-margin, everyday low prices?

The average turnover rate among retailers in the U.S. is 66.1 percent, according to the National Retail Federation. At Wal-Mart—where the turnover rate is about 55 percent—ambitious growth plans will be slowed by a lack of people. Wal-Mart has plenty of capital for the expansion, but not enough warm bodies to work those new stores. By way of comparison, Costco is well-known for taking good care of its workers, who, in turn, have been loyal to the company. Costco's warehouse workers start with an hourly wage of at least $10. After four years with the company, a cashier can earn around $44,000, including bonuses. Its turnover rate is just 23 percent.

The people challenge will be even greater for category killers in specialized areas. For example, Home Depot and Lowe's need people with product expertise and construction experience. As Home Depot moves farther and farther from its entrepreneurial roots, it will be difficult to find people who buy into their system and "bleed orange." Ever-growing stock shares enabled the early employees of Home Depot and Wal-Mart to get rich; that's never going to happen to a new employee at a mature company.

In early 2004, when Home Depot wanted to hire thirty-five thousand new employees, the do-it-yourself category killer formed a partnership with AARP (formerly known as the

American Association of Retired Persons) to hire skilled workers
for a variety of in-store positions, including plumbers, electri-
cians, landscapers, and sales and customer sales representatives
through the AARP Foundation Senior Community Service Em-
ployment Program, which will help to provide a pool of qualified low-income workers aged fifty-five and older. Older workers generally stay with a company longer and have a good
understanding of customer service.

The Future

Category killers offer more products in their classification than
could ever have been found in a general merchandise store or a
department store. They have driven out the inefficient or un-
competitive retailers, and they have enabled virtually every
consumer product to be affordable to middle-class shoppers.

While critics contend that these retailers destroyed our
mom-and-pop culture, there is more to the story. Granted,
many mom-and-pops have gone by the wayside (for a wide
variety of reasons). But, after all is said and done, Staples,
Costco, and some of the other big-box stores have also been a
boon to small-business owners because they offer every product and service required to run their companies. These category killers have leveled the playing field to enable even the
smallest enterprises to extend their reach from around the
corner to around the world.

As long as the American population remains restless and
migratory, category killers—at least in the short term—will
continue to grow and be a part of the landscape, be it Mesa,
Arizona or New York, New York. They will continue to thrive
in their categories because of their enormous buying power,
product assortment, and sharp pricing.

Ten years from now, will category killers be as dominant as
they are today? The answer to that question will depend on
how these retailers meet the challenges of the marketplace—

and in what particular product category they operate. Like department stores in the early 1980s and traditional discount stores in the early 1990s, category killers will have to protect their market share from other channels of distribution, including the Internet, general merchandise discounters, warehouse clubs, existing retailers who have adjusted to the times, and upstart retailers within their existing category that have come up with fresh new ideas and approaches. Take for example Metal Supermarkets, which sells all sorts of metals in small quantities (no minimum orders) to individual customers. The self-proclaimed "convenience store of the metals industry" opened its first store in 1985 and attracts customers who can't find the particular stainless steel or aluminum piece they need at Home Depot or Lowe's, which can't equal Metal Supermarkets' commitment to depth and breadth of product inventory. Then there's the Container Store, a 30-unit chain that sells containers of all types, from boxes and bins to bottles and backpacks. Virtually every product category offered by the Container Store can be found at any number of category killers, such as Bed Bath & Beyond or Lowe's, but not in the depth of offerings or accompanied by its employees' product expertise. Concepts such as Metal Supermarket and the Container Store represent the beauty and the danger of retailing—the beauty of the unceasing resourcefulness of entrepreneurs, and the danger of ultimately destroying their competitors.

So category killers are not ensured of another tomorrow. To the extent that they adapt or tweak or fine-tool or reorganize they will continue to be vital and important to the consuming public, who are the final arbiters of retail survival. Otherwise, like the retail dinosaurs that once ruled the American retail landscape—Montgomery Ward, Kmart, and others—they will slowly fade from the scene, replaced by newcomers who best capture the contemporary needs of the consumer culture.

Notes

Chapter 1

1. Nancy E. Cohen, *America's Marketplace: The History of Shopping Centers* (Lyme, CT: Greenwich Publishing Group, Inc., 2002), 34.

Chapter 2

1. "Keynote for 1929," *Toy World* 25 (December 1928).

2. Robert Spector, *More Than A Store: Frederick & Nelson 1890–1990* (Seattle: Documentary Book Publishers, 1990).

3. David Owen, "Where Toys Come From: Selling fun to children is one of capitalism's least predictable pursuits," *Atlantic Monthly*, October 1986.

4. Penrose Scull, with Prescott C. Fuller, *From Peddlers to Merchant Princes: A History of Selling in America* (Chicago: Follett Publishing Company, 1967), 247.

5. Tedlow, Richard, *New and Improved: The Story of Mass Marketing in America* (New York: Basic Books, 1990).

6. Robert Hendrickson, *The Grand Emporiums: The Illustrated History of America's Great Department Stores* (New York: Stein and Day, 1979) 256.

7. The following story is taken largely from *When Giants Stumble: Classic Business Blunders and How to Avoid Them* (Paramus, N.J.: Prentice Hall, 1999) by Robert Sobel.

8. <http://pages.emerson.edu/students/wan_wen_huang/document/final_kmart.doc> (accessed 12 December 2003).

9. Sam Walton with John Huey, *Sam Walton: Made in America; My Story* (New York: Doubleday, 1992), 108–110.

10. Kurt Barnard, interview by author, 14 March 2003.

11. Bernard Loomis, interview with author, 1 April 2004.

12. Nanette Byrnes, "Toy Story: Old stores, new rivals, and changing trends have hammered Toys 'R' Us. Can CEO John Eyler Fix the Chain?" *BusinessWeek*, 4 December 2000, 129.

13. Loomis interview.

14. Owen, "Where Toys Come From."

15. Bob Ortega, *In Sam We Trust: The Untold Story of Sam Walton and How Wal-Mart Is Devouring America* (New York: Times Business, 1998), 135.

Chapter 3

1. I. Jeanne Dugan, "The Baron of Books," *BusinessWeek*, 29 June 1998.

2. Ibid.

3. Ibid.

4. Robert Spector, *Amazon.com: Get Big Fast* (New York: Harper-Business, 2000).

5. Patrick M. Reilly, "Street Fighters: Where Borders Group and Barnes & Noble Compete, It's a War; Book Chains Find Themselves Pulling Out Stops to Win Soul of the Urban Reader," *Wall Street Journal*, 3 September 1996, A1.

6. Jeffrey A. Trachtenberg, "The Problem in Aisle One," *Wall Street Journal*, 16 August 2002, B1.

7. Bernie Marcus and Arthur Blank, with Bob Andelman, *Built from Scratch: How a Couple of Regular Guys Grew The Home Depot from Nothing to $30 Billion* (New York: Times Business, 1999), 81.

8. Ibid.

9. Patricia Sellers, "Exit the Builder, Enter the Repairman," *Fortune,* March 19, 2001; <www.fortune.com/fortune/subs/print/O,15935, 369599,00.html> (accessed July 21, 2004).

10. Paco Underhill, *Why We Buy: The Science of Shopping* (New York: Touchstone, 1999), 121–123.

11. Thomas G. Stemberg, *Staples for Success: From Business Plan to Billion-Dollar Business in Just a Decade* (Santa Monica, California: Knowledge Exchange, 1996), 2–8.

12. Ibid., 36.

13. Ibid., 18.

14. Lynne Adams, interview by author, December 2001.

15. Ibid.

16. Michael V. Copeland, "Best Buy's Selling Machine," *Business 2.0,* July 2004, 93.

17. Stanley Holmes et al., "Planet Starbucks," *BusinessWeek*, 9 September 2002, 100.

18. Andy Serwer, "Hot Starbucks to Go," *Fortune*, 25 January 2004.

19. Sam Walton with John Huey, *Sam Walton: Made in America; My Story* (New York: Doubleday, 1992), 80.

Chapter 4

1. "The WWD List: Lifestyles of the Super Wealthy," *Women's Wear Daily*, 3 June 2004, 12.

2. Steven Greenhouse, "Wal-Mart Driving Workers and Supermarkets Crazy," *New York Times*, 19 October 2003.

3. Gary M. Stibel, founder and partner, New England Consulting Group, interview by author, 1 July 2004.

4. Murray Krieger, *The Complete Dictionary of Buying and Merchandising* (New York: National Retail Merchants Association, 1987), 78.

5. Timothy J. Mullaney, "Deck the Halls with High-Speed Access," *BusinessWeek*, 8 December 2003.

6. Cate T. Corcoran, "Wal-Mart Details RFID to Top Suppliers," *Women's Wear Daily*, 18 June 2004.

7. Greg Buzek, interview by author, 5 November 2003.

8. "Circuit City Stores Will Offer Private-Label Brand Products," *Wall Street Journal*, 31 March 2004.

9. David Stires, "Is Your Store a Bank in Drag?" *Fortune*, 4 March 2003.

10. Matthew Boyle, "Brand Killers," *Fortune*, 21 July 2003.

11. Caroline E. Mayer, "Happy Campers at the Store: Retailers Find Summer Kids Programs Pay Off," *Washington Post*, 12 July 2003, 1.

12. Jeffrey A. Trachtenberg, "Barnes & Noble Pushes Books from Ambitious Publisher: Itself," *Wall Street Journal*, 18 June 2003.

13. Ibid.

14. Hillel Italie, "Borders Program Protested," *Detroit Free Press*, June 27, 2002.

Chapter 5

1. Penrose Scull, with Prescott C. Fuller, *From Peddlers to Merchant Princes: A History of Selling in America* (Chicago: Follett Publishing Company, 1967), 247.

2. Carol Mongo, "Le Bon Marché," *Paris Voice*, May 2002.

3. Ibid; Elaine Showalter, *Emile Zola, Au Bonheur des Dames (The Ladies' Paradise)*, (New York: Penguin Books, 1995–2000).

4. Mongo, "Le Bon Marché."

5. Nancy E. Cohen, *America's Marketplace: The History of Shopping Centers* (Lyme, CT: Greenwich Publishing Group, Inc., 2002), 34.

6. Ibid., 35.

7. Robert Hendrickson, *The Grand Emporiums: The Illustrated History of America's Great Department Stores* (New York: Stein and Day, 1979), 273.

8. Robert DiNicola, interview by author, 20 August 2003.

9. Evan Clark, "The Target Squeeze: Chain Battles Foes: From Above and Below," *Women's Wear Daily*, 27 January 2003.

10. Jon E. Hilsenrath, "Retailers Score Points in Keeping Consumers Happy," *Wall Street Journal*, 19 February 2002.

11. Amy Merrick, Jeffrey A. Trachtenberg, and Ann Zimmerman, "Idle Aisles: Department Stores Fight an Uphill Battle Just to Stay Relevant," *Wall Street Journal*, 12 March 2002, A1.

12. Dan Burrows, "Broadline Stats: Discounters Gaining," *Women's Wear Daily*, 7 January 2004.

13. Paco Underhill, *Why We Buy: The Science of Shopping* (New York: Touchstone, 1999), 121–123.

14. Robert Mang, interview by author, 26 August 2003.

15. Tony Margolis, interview by author, 20 August 2003.

16. Donald R. Katz, *The Big Store: Inside The Crisis and Revolution at Sears* (New York: Penguin Books, 1987), 10.

17. Amy Merrick, Jeffrey A. Trachtenberg, and Ann Zimmerman, "Idle Aisles: Department Stores Fight an Uphill Battle Just to Stay Relevant."

18. Walter Loeb, interview by author, 19 April 2002.

19. Robert Berner, "Dark Days in White Goods for Sears," *BusinessWeek*, 10 March 2003.

Chapter 6

1. Kortney Stringer, "Abandoning the Mall," *Wall Street Journal*, 24 March 2004; Author query to International Council of Shopping Centers, July 1, 2004, to verify data.

2. Kemper Freeman, interview by author, 17 December 2002.

3. Ibid.

4. Merritt Sher, interview by author, 21 March 2004.

5. Louise Lee, "Thinking Small at the Mall," *BusinessWeek*, 29 May 2003.

6. Leslie Earnest, "Almighty Dollar Stores Rake in Billions," *Los Angeles Times* (reprinted in *The Seattle Times*), 9 April 2004.

7. Sharon Edelson, "Dollar Stores Gain Momentum," *Women's Wear Daily*, 23 February 2004.

8. Earnest, "Almighty Dollar Stores"; Edelson, "Dollar Stores Gain Momentum."

9. Michael Brick, "Seeking Customers in a Blighted Area," *New York Times*, 12 February 2003.

Chapter 7

1. Joseph H. Ellis, interview by author, 2 September 2003.

2. Sharon Edelson, "Wal-Mart's Future: Will It Become Engine of the U.S. Economy?" *Women's Wear Daily*, 21 August 2003.

3. Dan Morse, "New Home Depot Office in China Will Focus on Establishing Stores," *Wall Street Journal*, 8 June 2004.

4. Ken Belson, "As Starbucks Grows, Japan, Too is Awash," *New York Times*, 21 October 2001.

Chapter 8

1. Kristin Young, "ICSC: A Conclave of Concerns," *Women's Wear Daily,* 28 May 2003, 2.

2. Jake Batsell, "When Giant Wal-Mart Knocks, There's a Town Battle in Store," *Seattle Times*, 28 July 2002.

3. Michael Beyard, interview by author, 20 August 2003.

4. *Berman v. Parker*, 348 U.S. 26, 33 (1954).

5. Donald J. Kochan, "Public v. Private Uses, Mackinac Center for Public Policy," April 15, 1996, <http://www.mackinac.org> (accessed December 4, 2003).

6. Dana Berliner, *Public Power, Private Gain: A Five-Year, State-By-State Report Examining the Abuse of Eminent Domain* (Washington, DC: Institute For Justice, 2003), 4.

7. Ibid., 218.

8. Dana Berliner, interview by author, 9 May 2004.

9. <http://www.empire.state.ny.us/> (accessed 4 March 2004).

10. Alex Halperin. "Condeming (for) Private Business"; *New York (NY) Gotham Gazette,* 4 March 2002.

11. Martha L. Willman, "Lancaster Ready to Put Parkland in a Big Box Business," *Los Angeles Times*, 24 June 2001.

12. Steven Greenhut, "Costco's Big-Box Political Clout," *Santa Ana (CA) Orange County Register*, 23 June 2002.

13. Maggie Gallagher, "The Lord Giveth, Costco Taketh Away," 14 August 2002, <http://www.townhall.com> (accessed 4 April 2004).

14. Ramesh Ponnura, "This Land is Costco's Land: Cities Steal Property, and Give it to Costco," *National Review Online*, 18 February 2003, <http://www.nationalreview.com>.

15. Malcolm R. Riley, interview by author, 26 August 2003.

16. Sharon Edelson, "Wal-Mart's Future: Will It Become Engine of the U.S. Economy?" *Women's Wear Daily*, 21 August 2003.

17. Terry Pristin, "Abandoned Space, the Final Frontier? Hey, It's a Whole Other Business," *New York Times*, 16 June 2004.

18. Charles Fishman, "The Wal-Mart You Don't Know," *Fast Company*, December 2003; Abigail Goldman and Nancy Cleeland, "Wal-Mart's empire reshaping workplace," *Los Angeles Times,* published in *Seattle Times*, November 27, 2003; Steven Greenhouse, "Wal-Mart, A Nation unto Itself," *New York Times*, 17 April 2004; Jerry Useem, "Should We Admire Wal-Mart?" *Fortune*, 23 February 2004.

19. Kristin Young, "L.A. Proposes SuperCenter Restrictions," *Women's Wear Daily*, 19 December 2003.

20. Pam Belluck, "Presevationists Call Vermont Endangered, by Wal-Mart," *New York Times*, 25 May 2004, A22.

21. <http://www.fundersnetwork.org> (accessed 4 January 2003).

22. Peter Corroon, interview by author, 28 October 2003.

23. Mike Kaszuba, "City Pushes to Secede From 'Starbucks Nation,'" *Minneapolis Star-Tribune,* July 20, 2003, 20.

24. Jake Batsell, "Starbucks Turned a Shot into a Grande," *Seattle Times*, 4 November 2001.

25. Kaszuba, "City Pushes to Secede."

26. Cora Daniels, "Mr. Coffee: The Man Behind the $4.75 Frappuccino Makes the 500," *Fortune*, 14 April 2003.

27. Breathing Planet <http://www.breathingplanet.net/whirl/> (accessed 4 April 2004).

28. Pat Sullivan, interview by author, 4 November 2003.

29. Membership records from 1990–2004, American Booksellers Association.

30. Collette Morgan, interview by author, 6 November 2003.

31. Bill Hibler, interview by author, 15 November 2003.

Chapter 9

1. David Brooks, "Our Sprawling Supersize Utopia," *The New York Times Magazine*, 4 April 2004, 46.

2. Ibid.

3. Brian Libby, "Can Old Malls Be Taught New Tricks?" *New York Times*, 15 June 2003.

4. Michael Beyard, interview by author, 30 August 2003.

5. Richard Green, interview by author, 7 May 2004.

6. David Moin and Kristin Young, "Breaking Ground on Fresh Shopping Venues," *Women's Wear Daily*, 7 June 2004, 8.

7. Alan Doerschel, interview by author, 4 May 2004.

8. Nanette Byrnes, "Toy Story: Old stores, new rivals, and changing trends have hammered Toys "R" Us. Can CEO John Eyler Fix the Chain?" *BusinessWeek*, 4 December, 2000, 129.

9. Bernie Marcus and Arthur Blank, with Bob Andelman, *Built from Scratch: How a Couple of Regular Guys Grew The Home Depot from Nothing to $30 Billion* (New York: Times Business, 1999), 260.

10. Dan Morse, "Home Depot Is Struggling To Adjust to New Blueprint," *Wall Street Journal*, 17 January 2003.

11. Home Depot Annual Report 2003.

Bibliography

Publications

Barmash, Isadore. *Macy's For Sale: The Leveraged Buyout of The World's Largest Store*. New York: Weidenfeld & Nicolson, 1989.

Beaumont, Constance E. *Better Models for Superstores: Alternatives to Big-Box Sprawl*. Washington, DC: National Trust for Historic Preservation, 1997.

Beaumont, Constance E., ed. *Challenging Sprawl: Organizational Responses to a National Problem*. Washington, DC: National Trust for Historic Preservation, 1999.

Berliner, Dana. *Public Power, Private Gain: A Five-Year, State-By-State Report Examining the Abuse of Eminent Domain*. Washington, DC: Institute for Justice, 2003.

Chuihua, Judy Chung, Jeffrey Inaba, Rem Koolhaas, and Sze Tsung Leong, editors. *Project on the City: The Harvard Design School Guide to Shopping*. Köln, Germany: Taschen GmbH, 2001.

Cohen, Lizabeth. *A Consumers' Republic: The Politics of Mass Consumption in Postwar America*. New York: Alfred A. Knopf, 2003.

Cohen, Nancy E. *America's Marketplace: The History of Shopping Centers*. Lyme, CT: Greenwich Publishing Group, Inc., 2002.

Cross, Gary. An All-Consuming Century: Why Commercialism Won in Modern America. *New York: Columbia University Press, 2003*.

Ferry, John William. *A History of the Department Store*. New York: Macmillan, 1960.

Harris, Leon A. *Merchant Prices: An Intimate History of Jewish Families Who Built Great Department Stores*. Harper & Row, New York, 1979.

Hendrickson, Robert. *The Grand Emporiums: The Illustrated History of America's Great Department Stores*. New York: Stein and Day, 1979.

Jackson, Kenneth T. *Crabgrass Frontier: The Suburbanization of the United States*. New York: Oxford University Press, 1985.

Katz, Donald R. *The Big Store: Inside The Crisis and Revolution at Sears*. New York: Penguin, 1987.

Kowinski, William Severini. *The Malling of America: An Inside Look at the Great Consumer Paradise*. New York: William Morrow and Company, Inc., 1985.

Leach, William. *Land of Desire: Merchants, Power, and the Rise of a New American Culture*. New York: Pantheon Books, 1993.

Marcus, Bernie, and Arthur Blank, with Bob Andelman. *Built From Scratch: How a Couple of Regular Guys Grew The Home Depot from Nothing to $30 Billion*. New York: Times Business, 1999.

Norman, Al. *Slam-Dunking Wal-Mart: How You Can Stop Superstore Sprawl in Your Hometowns*. Atlantic City, NJ: Raphel Marketing, 1999.

Ortega, Bob. *In Sam We Trust: The Untold Story of Sam Walton and How Wal-Mart Is Devouring America*. New York: Times Business, 1998.

Quinn, Bill. *How Wal-Mart Is Destroying America (and the World) and What You Can Do About It*. Berkeley, CA: Ten Speed Press, 2000.

Schultz, Howard and Dori Jones Yang. *Pour Your Heart Into It: How Starbucks Built a Company One Cup at a Time*. New York: Hyperion, 1997.

Scull, Penrose, with Prescott C. Fuller. *From Peddlers to Merchant Princes: A History of Selling in America*. Chicago: Follett Publishing Company, 1967.

Sobel, Robert. *When Giants Stumble: Classic Business Blunders and How to Avoid Them*. Paramus, NJ: Prentice Hall, 1999.

Spector, Robert. *Amazon.com: Get Big Fast*. New York: HarperBusiness, 2000.

Spector, Robert. *More Than A Store: Frederick & Nelson 1890–1990*. Seattle: Documentary Book Publishers, 1990.

Stemberg, Thomas G. *Staples For Success: From Business Plan to Billion-Dollar Business in Just a Decade*. Santa Monica, CA: Knowledge Exchange, 1996.

Trimble, Vance H. *Sam Walton, Founder of Wal-Mart: The Inside Story of America's Richest Man*. New York: Penguin, 1990.

Underhill, Paco. *Why We Buy: The Science of Shopping*. New York: Touchstone, 1999.

Walton, Sam, with John Huey. *Sam Walton: Made in America; My Story.* New York: Doubleday, 1992.

Wood, Robert E., *Mail Order Retailing: Pioneered in Chicago* (New York: Newcomen Society, 1948): 9. Cited in Richard Tedlow, *New and Improved: The Story of Mass Marketing in America* (New York: Basic Books, 1990): 272.

Author Interviews

All of the following parties were interviewed by the author, either in person or via telephone in the period from January 2002 through May 2004.

Lynne Adams, PETsMART
Kurt Barnard, Barnard's Retail Trend Report
Dana Berliner, Institute for Justice
Willard Bishop, Willard Bishop Consulting
Michael Beyard, Urban Land Institute
Greg Buzek, IHL Consulting Group
Peter Corroon, Salt Lake Vest Pocket Business Coalition
Wendall Cox, independent consultant
Susan Detmer, CBRichard Ellis
Robert DiNicola, retired chairman, Zale Corporation
Alan Doerschel, City of Tukwila
Joseph H. Ellis, Goldman Sachs
Mason Frank, MBK Northwest
Kemper Freeman, Bellevue Square
Richard Green, Westfield Holdings
Krista Haverly, CB Richard Ellis
Bill Hibler, Quidnunc
Richard Latella, Cushman & Wakefield
Wendy Leibmann, WSL Strategic Retail
Walter Loeb, Loeb Associates
Bernard Loomis, toy industry consultant
Robert Mang, department store executive
Tony Margolis, Tommy Bahama
Collette Morgan, Wild Rumpus
Milt Reimers, CB Richard Ellis
Malcolm R. Riley, Malcolm Riley & Associates
Gregg Rosenberg, Beverly's Pets

Michael Sandorffy, developer
Merritt Sher, Terranomics Development
Carl Steidtmann, Deloitte Research
Gary M. Stibel, New England Consulting Group
Pat Sullivan, Sullivan's Hardware
Gary Volchok, CB Richard Ellis

Index

About the Author

ROBERT SPECTOR writes and speaks about retailing, customer service, and corporate culture. His books include *The Nordstrom Way: The Inside Story of America's #1 Customer Service Company*; *Amazon.Com: Get Big Fast*, and *Anytime, Anywhere: How the Best Bricks-and-Clicks Businesses Deliver Seamless Service to Their Customers*. His work has appeared in many publications, including the *Wall Street Journal*, the *New York Times*, and *Women's Wear Daily*.

Spector speaks to a wide variety of corporations and organizations throughout the world. His presentations focus on how organizations can create a corporate culture that emphasizes outstanding customer service.

A native of Perth Amboy, New Jersey, and a graduate of Franklin & Marshall College, he resides in Seattle with his wife, Marybeth, and their daughter, Fae.

Visit his Web site: www.robertspector.com.